THE SENSE OF HIS PRESENCE

DAVID R.
MAINS

THE SENSE OF HIS PRESENCE

Experiencing
Spiritual
Regenesis

WORD PUBLISHING
Dallas · London · Vancouver · Melbourne

THE SENSE OF HIS PRESENCE

Unless otherwise noted, Scripture quotations are from The Revised Standard Version of the Bible (RSV), copyrighted 1946, 1952, © 1971, 1973 by the Division of Christian Education of the National Council of the Churches of Christ in the U.S.A., and are used by permission. Scriptures marked NIV are from The Holy Bible, New International Version; copyright © 1973, 1978, 1984 International Bible Society, used by permission of Zondervan Bible Publishers. Scriptures marked KJV are from the King James Version of the Bible

Acknowledgment for other copyrighted material used in this book begins p. 190

Library of Congress Cataloging-in-Publication Data:

Mains, David R.
  The sense of his presence

  Bibliography: p. 183
  1. Church renewal. 2. Spiritual life. I. Title.
BV600.2.M342   1988   269   88-5436
ISBN 0-8499-3107-X

Printed in the United States of America

        0 1 2 3 9   RRD   9 8 7 6 5 4 3

To my second son,

JOEL

named after the prophet who wrote:
Return to the Lord your God,
for he is gracious and compassionate,
slow to anger
and abounding in love
(Joel 2:13, NIV)

Contents

Introduction

WHEN A CHURCH is at its very best—your church or any church—it is always marked by an overwhelming sense of Christ's presence. This sense of His presence is also the outstanding characteristic of times of genuine revival in the church. And I believe it is the standard for church success that needs to be rediscovered in this generation.

But a phrase like "an overwhelming sense of Christ's presence in the church" can sound a bit abstract. A way to make it more concrete is to ask: "What would happen in a church if Christ was bodily a part of the congregation?"

Answering this question does two things. First, it nails down specifics as to what is truly important in the church. Second, it helps us understand what the best of times in Christ's church have been like. That's because we learn from history that the things that would happen if Christ came to His church are the very marks of classic revivals—those times in history when God's presence has been most acutely felt.

My approach in this book, then, is simple. It is my desire to help both clergy and laity see what would occur if Jesus himself was physically a part of their congregation. Then I remind readers that Christ is always present as Lord of His church—it's just that He must be seen through eyes of faith.

To make all of this more real, after each chapter I have provided readings from my library that paint a picture of what it's like when a body of believers sense the presence of the Lord. Some of these are first-hand accounts from significant times of revival down through the centuries. Others are relevant quotes from respected revival leaders or scholars on this subject. I hope these will give you a feel of what it is like to experience the sense of His presence.

I'm interested in more than understanding, however. So at the end of each chapter I have also included a series of questions for personal reflection or small-group discussion. These questions are designed to help you apply the topics covered in this book—so that you actually begin to experience a renewed sense of the Lord's presence in your life and church. I hope you will consider them seriously.

My prayer is that there will also be passion in these pages. I don't want this to be the kind of emotion you feel when a preacher has you cornered and now he's shaking his fist and starting to holler. But I do want you to be aware that my heart truly longs for what I'm describing. And I hold a conviction that this is where God's heart is as well. If it sounds good to you also, another great day of His presence could be closer than is usually thought.

Wouldn't that be something?!

A Scenario

IT'S SUNDAY MORNING, and you're in church.

Sunlight streams in through the windows, and the organist is playing a prelude. All is hushed and reverent (except for the two people behind you carrying on a conversation and the sounds of traffic going by outside).

Suddenly, there He is, sitting on a chair by the pulpit.

At first, not everyone sees Him. But quickly, by whispers and nudges, all are soon made aware.

"Look who's sitting on the platform!"

"Could it be?"

"I'm sure it is—the scars on His hands—it has to be—it's Jesus . . . !"

And what will happen next? . . .

1

The Standard

— ◆ —

H OW DO YOU MEASURE the spiritual life of a church?

Put differently, how can you tell whether the Body is on the right track, functioning as our Lord intends it to function?

This is a question both lay people and ministers ask, although the phraseology varies.

People in the pew might wonder, "Would the church across town be better for my teens?" "Is it worth it to drive forty-five minutes on Sunday morning to worship in a setting I really appreciate?" "When the family moves, how should we choose a new church?"

And ministers ask themselves, "How can I tell whether I'm doing a good job?" "Should I stay at this church, or should I move on?" "What are the right measurements for success in the church, anyway?"

One pastor friend and I talked about this recently as we discussed his quandary whether or not to accept a call from another church. "It's a bigger congregation and probably in a better location, but for some reason I'm just not sure the Lord wants me to take it."

"Describe for me what you see as the perfect church situation for you," I replied.

His answer was almost immediate. "I know where my heart is. I want to pastor a church that experiences revival."

My interest was instantly aroused. Revival is a subject I've studied all my adult life. But when I ask my colleagues how they would identify revival if they experienced it, I find that most get lost in muddy definitions.

So I challenged my pastor friend with the approach I have developed over these years of study.

"What would happen," I asked, "if Jesus came to your church this Sunday—I mean, if He were physically present?"

He was surprised by my question, but he only had to think

a minute: "My people would probably drop to their knees and worship Him!" he said.

"What else?"

"Well, I guess they would be more loving . . ."

"And? . . ."

"They'd sure take sin a lot more seriously . . ."

My pastor friend became more animated as his imagination began to grasp the picture I had been suggesting. "If Christ were bodily here in our church, I could see my people really getting excited about serving Him! . . ."

Together we brainstormed other changes that would occur if Christ were physically present in His church—a new and eager desire to talk to the Lord in prayer and a matching urgency to heed carefully His words to us; an excitement about sharing the realities of the Lord's presence with non-Christians; and, finally, a growing conviction that life in His presence was the best life possible.

Suddenly our conversation took an unexpected turn as I heard my minister friend say, "Hey! I just discovered my answer about how to respond to that offer from the bigger church."

I was intrigued. "What do you mean?"

"I'm supposed to stay where I am!"

And then he explained: "Everything we've just been talking about—it's starting to happen! Worship is just beginning to be understood, but it's coming. And my people are demonstrably loving one another; just recently, several bad relationships were made right. Then, in the last months, there have been tears of repentance—the emphasis on holiness we talked about. Almost all in my congregation are actively involved in service of one kind or another. Our prayer meeting is growing steadily, and my people are responding beautifully to the group Bible studies I've started. Then, it seems like we have conversions almost every week.

"Now I know why I've been reluctant to leave. Ministry here has been too good. But more than that, I just realized that we must be experiencing early signs of revival. My ideal situation is right where I am! I'd be crazy to leave!"

This pastor was absolutely right. But why hadn't he seen earlier the value of what was happening in his church? Probably because he, like many, had never thought of this simple way to measure it. A common problem for pastors and parishioners alike is that a majority of them are confused as to how to evaluate a church's ministry. They're just not sure what the standards should be.

For example, is size an accurate way to judge whether a particular church is "successful"? Not necessarily; numbers can fool you!

A lot of people think of the physical structure when they hear the word *church;* to them, a beautiful sanctuary equals a beautiful church. And it's true that buildings have great appeal to both clergy and laity, especially if they're also in the right location. But it's also true that in many cities there are breathtaking church structures which over the years have become little more than museums.

Then there's the question of budget—maybe an enormous budget is a good indication that a church's ministry is effective. But there are believers who can testify to attending high-budget churches whose members lived decidedly unchristian lives!

What about doctrinal purity? It's unthinkable that the people in a church with pure doctrine (written carefully into the constitution) would be less than all that Christ would expect. But right doctrine, of course, was the Pharisees' hallowed test, to which they added a few refinements of their own!

"Does the church meet my needs?" That's a popular measurement among lay people. Perhaps your local church does meet your needs—but then maybe your needs are really of little consequence when compared to the underlying reasons why Christ established His church here on earth! A person may need to make some new business or social contacts, for example, but that is hardly why the Lord founded His church.

Here's another common statement people make when considering their church preference: "I like the pastor. I like the staff. They're very outgoing, friendly, and approachable."

(Or, "I like the congregation; they are friendly and appreciative of my ministry.") Actually, friendliness may or may not have a bearing on true spirituality. Some of the friendliest people I know are not even Christians!

How about the rich historical tradition of a given church? (What about the *present* history? It may be utterly lousy.) Or how about prestige, educational achievement, financial status, the cultural level? If we are honest, we have to admit that these standards have more to do with the secularized community, the research statisticians, the media pollsters, or just plain personal taste than with spiritual values.

So, how can the ministry and life of a church be measured? What are the marks of a truly successful church?

In my mind, the answers revolve around a single standard: *Is there a strong, abiding sense of the presence of the Lord here?*

More specifically, do the people perceive this presence of Christ to the degree that they come prepared truly to worship Him—or do they just go through Sunday morning motions?

Is Christian love expressed in such a remarkable way that all can see the living Christ is truly present among His people? Or are the relationships as flawed, as petty, as hateful as in the general society around us?

Is victory over sin a quality which consistently marks the people at all levels—adults, teens, even grade-schoolers?

Are the people in this church excited about the privilege they have as subjects of the King to serve Him?

Are they eager to learn more of the Scriptures and to hear them taught? Are Bible studies full? Is there enthusiasm about personal application of the Word?

Do the people see value in spending quality time talking to Christ? Is there evidence of prayer cells forming? Are believers comfortable about asking each other to pray?

Are church members sharing with others the news that their Lord is truly in their midst? Do they seek for ways to include, invite, welcome outsiders into the life of the church?

And is there a general sense of well-being, a feeling that life in the church is as God intended it to be; in fact, that

18

living with Christ in the midst of His people is the best life possible on this earth?

These eight indicators seem to me to be extremely helpful measurements by which we can evaluate the spiritual life in a church. Twenty people in a storefront with Christ in their midst is much preferable to two thousand in a cathedral where the Lord's presence is not sought and valued. And if His presence is valued, neither number is as important as that reality.

The sense of His presence—this is a most satisfactory criterion on which to base our church goals and planning. It is a wise standard for evaluating to which churches we give our allegiance, time, talents, and financial support. It is also a sure rule by which professionals can measure their commitment and job choices.

In business, the bottom line may be profit; in professional sports, success means winning; in television, it's the ratings; in politics, votes.

But in the church, it's the presence of the Lord that's all important.

But Christ *is* always present in His church, isn't He? Hasn't He promised to be in our midst whenever two or more of us gather in His name?

So why aren't all churches like what has just been described?

Unfortunately, as the Old and New Testament prophets put it, too often "we have eyes to see and do not see, ears to hear and do not hear." And so we carry out business as usual in our churches, forgetting that the Lord *is* with us as He promised to be.

And the result is churches that are markedly less than what Christ intended His church to be, congregations that go through the motions without a clear sense of who they are supposed to be or what they are supposed to do, local bodies that pick up their agenda from the culture around them instead of marching to Christ's drum.

And that's why we need revival . . .

19

Now, when I write about *revival,* I am not thinking of the one- or two-week evangelistic meetings dubbed "revivals" in many churches—although I suppose revival could happen in such a setting. And I don't have in mind emotionalism or hellfire-and-brimstone preaching—although times of revival often involve deep emotion and convicting sermons.

When I refer to genuine revival, I mean those seasons in the life of a church, a region, a nation—or even an individual— when there is a fresh awareness of Christ's presence. During such times, it's as though our Lord takes the veil that normally hides Himself from us and draws it back more than we expect, so that we experience Him—not totally, but certainly in a wonderfully new and overpowering way.

Sometimes I prefer to use the word *regenesis* for this experience instead of *revival.* It doesn't have as many negative connotations. To me, *regenesis* speaks of a new beginning, a return to the closeness humankind first enjoyed with the Creator in the Garden of Eden. Whatever the word, revival or regenesis is a time when people discover with dramatic newness the reality and power of Christ's presence in their midst.

And so when I ask, "What are the marks of spiritual success in a church?" I am also asking, "What are the signs of revival in a local church, the church in a large geographic area, or even Christ's church in an entire nation or continent?" The questions are slightly different, but the measurements are the same—for revival, like the church when it is right on target and knowing spiritual success, is marked most of all by that powerful and unmistakable awareness that Christ has again drawn wonderfully close.

But we must always force ourselves to define what that closeness results in, or the word *revival* gradually takes on an almost mystical meaning of its own. For example, I was recently in a small group where a fellow preacher told about the events at a church where he had just spent a week as guest preacher. It had been a wonderful time of renewal, and the Lord's presence had certainly been felt. There had been reconciliation between warring parties. Restitution for past wrongs had been made by some of the members. "It was like revival!" the man stated excitedly.

"No!" responded another in the group emphatically. "It couldn't have been revival. You can't explain revival. I can explain everything you've been talking about. Genuine revival is so marvelous there's no way it can be explained in human terms."

Well—I strongly disagree! There's no question in my mind but what revival is wonderfully supernatural. And it's true that we can't predict exactly what the Holy Spirit will do.

But this doesn't mean evaluation is impossible—that there's no way to measure the unique mixture of the natural and the supernatural, the human and the divine that will always mark this experience. (This book is an attempt to suggest some of those measurements.) And it certainly doesn't mean we can do nothing to prepare ourselves to again know revival, to work at becoming freshly aware of the sense of His presence!

In fact, I believe preparation for revival is important and necessary. That's why I guard against what I call the legend and lore of revival, which can lead us off track. For example, some say that revival comes suddenly and mysteriously and there is little we can do about it—except possibly pray for it. Too often, when describing major revivals in the church, I fear that enthusiasts contribute to this mindset by using parlance like "the day the fire fell," or "when the rains finally came to this parched, dry land," and so on. (In fact, I'm guilty of this myself sometimes.) While it's true that there's a sense of suddenness when the full wake of revival is felt, it's also true that major revivals usually require periods of preparation before reaching full maturity.

Dr. J. Edwin Orr of Fuller Theological Seminary, who studied and wrote more on the subject of revival than any recent American scholar, confirmed this when I spoke with him before his death in 1987. I asked, "Does revival come all of a sudden, or is it more of a process?" His answer was "both"—that, in his opinion, revival usually builds up slowly (taking up to ten years for a nationwide revival), then has a "trigger point" when it seems to explode and spread rapidly.

History is replete with examples. The Protestant Reformation was one of the most significant times of revival in Western history. Its "trigger point" was Martin Luther's nailing his Ninety-five Theses to the church door in Wittenberg and, even more specifically, publicly burning the Papal bull which condemned his theological works.

December 10, 1520 at 9 A.M.—when Luther touched fire to the Papal bull at the town rubbish pit—can almost be seen as the specific moment when flames of revival began to blaze and a modern spiritual era began. But in a sense, the Reformation had been smoldering for years. In the previous century, such men as the German theologian, John of Wesel; the Dutch theologian, Wessel; the Italian Savanorola; and especially England's John Wycliffe and Bohemia's John Huss had begun the work of bringing new life to a despiritualized church. Without their preparations, the Reformation flames might never have caught.

So in a sense, there are these two aspects in the timing of revival—the longer preparation process and the sudden, visible trigger point. This is true both at the local level and in the larger church. And this timing is all-important. If the spark ignites prematurely, the revival will quickly burn itself out; it will last a few days, a few weeks maybe, and will be confined to a relatively small group of people. Instead of inspiring the kind of true repentance that changes individuals, families, churches, communities, and nations; the flame, if it comes too soon and without proper preparation, becomes only an emotional flare-up.

Sometimes, then, I find myself almost schizophrenic in my praying. "Lord, send revival soon!" I plead, then I hear myself saying, "But not too soon, Lord."

I am afraid that if reveille is blown prematurely, the troops will awaken and run to the battle ill-prepared. There must be wisdom regarding the strength of the enemy. There must be the protection that comes through holiness. There must be many mature leaders to give direction throughout the ranks when the battle is hot and heavy. And there must be a clear understanding of what victory looks like, or we won't recognize it when we experience it!

A wonderful old volume first published in 1846, entitled *New England Revivals As They Existed at the Close of the Eighteenth and the Beginning of the Nineteenth Centuries*, is a remarkable account of what genuine revival looks like. This book is basically the report from twenty-five pastors as to what happened to their churches during those special days we now refer to as the Second Great Awakening. The preface to this volume describes the kind of long-range, far-reaching revival I want for the churches of our generation:

> These revivals were not temporary excitements, which, like a tornado, sweep through a community, and leave desolations behind them; but they were like showers of rain, which refresh the dry and thirsty earth, and cause it to bring forth "herbs meet for them by whom it is dressed." These fruits were permanent. By them the churches were not only enlarged, but beautified and strengthened; and a benign influence was exerted upon the community around.[1]

Reading the chapter reports in this book, one gets the strong impression that these churches were restored to functioning in the basic way God intended them to function. New Testament Christianity, rather than subnormal Christianity, was being demonstrated. Startling accounts are sprinkled throughout the narratives, but these are the exception rather than the rule. The basic impression is of the church's strong forward move in strength and holiness and stability.

An account of what God did in Lenox, Massachusetts, as reported by Reverend Samuel Shepard, gives a feel for what I mean:

> At the time of my ordination, which was April, 1795, the situation of this church called for the earnest prayers of all who had a heart to pray. The number of its members then was not much greater than it had been for twenty-five years before; and almost the whole of them were bowing under the infirmities of

age. No person, who was in early life, was a member of this church. . . .

Such were the melancholy prospects of this church until the spring of the year 1799. While showers of divine grace were falling on other parts of Zion, and God, by his Spirit, was visiting one place and another, and quickening multitudes for his name's sake, we seemed to be solemnly warned in the words recorded, Rev. 2:5, "Remember therefore from whence thou art fallen, and repent . . . or else I will come unto thee quickly, and will remove thy candlestick out of his place."

In the month of April, 1799, several members of the church manifested great anxiety about the state of religion among us, and expressed a desire that meetings might be appointed for religious conference and special prayer for the outpouring of the Holy Spirit. A sermon was preached at this first meeting, and the audience were very attentive. At the next conference, we conversed upon a particular passage of Scripture, which led to a consideration of the being and perfections of God. Several persons at this meeting appeared unusually solemn. At the third conference meeting, were to be seen persons from every part of the town. The divine authority of the Scriptures was made the subject of conversation, and appearance of the assembly was truly affecting. They seemed now to consider the Holy Bible to be the very voice of God to a guilty world; and the religion of Jesus, a solemn reality. Sinners were brought to tremble in view of eternity, and [those who professed] religion were animated and rendered fervent in prayer. From that time, the work became more general— religious conferences were multiplied—and multitudes seemed to spare no pains in obtaining religious instruction. From that solemn season, there was an increasing attention to things of a serious nature, among young and old, for several months.

On the twentieth of October, twenty-four persons were received into the church. This was with us a memorable day. But a small part of the congregation had ever before seen a young person publicly engage in the Christian welfare. . . .

It was not till several months after this precious season that the attention began to abate. The whole number of who have been received into the church since the work began, is fifty-three. Many are in early life. Nearly all of them continue to give satisfactory evidence that Christ is, in reality, formed in them, the hope of glory.

May a holy God, in infinite mercy, continue to make manifest the glory of his power, and the glory of his grace, in building up Zion; for in no other way can we rationally hope to see happy individuals—happy families—happy neighborhoods—happy societies—happy towns—happy states—happy kingdoms—and a happy world.[2]

There is nothing sensational in that account—no fire from heaven, no unexplainable events. Yet Rev. Shepard, like the other contributors to the volume, was assuredly convinced he was part of a revival. I'm glad no one was there to say, "But this can't be true revival. I can explain everything you have told about. Genuine revival is so marvelous there's no way it can be explained in human terms."

One reason I am writing, then, is simply to underscore the common marks of genuine revival in the church so we will know it in its preparatory stages and know it as it begins to achieve a magnified impact among us. I believe God wants to surprise this generation with His presence. I hold a conviction that He is preparing His church for a new beginning, for a spiritual regenesis. Let us be aware of what it is we are seeking.

God is also a master at knowing when is the optimum time to pour out His Spirit on His people, and my personal belief is that this is yet a little in the future. What the present day calls for is the preparation of thousands of strong leaders all through the ranks who can properly propel this coming movement of the Spirit—pastors, teachers, youth leaders, evangelists, elders, lay workers, board members. Talent is not enough. Personality is no longer adequate. Appearance, money, or brains all fall short. What is needed in the ranks during revival is spiritual maturity.

The message we presently need to hear and proclaim is that reveille blast of John the Baptist: "Prepare ye the way of the Lord, make his paths straight" (Luke 3:4, KJV). A great day is ahead. Truly it will be a time when the Lord reveals Himself in a marvelous fashion. Start getting ready.

Several years ago, the Imperials, a Christian male quartet, put out an album with a song that became popular among the younger generation of believers. It goes like this:

> I listen to the trumpet of Jesus
>   While the world hears a different sound.
> I march to the drumbeat of God Almighty
>   While the others just wander around.
> I'm a member of the Holy Ghost traveling band.
>   I'm moving on up to a better land.
> I hear the voice of a supernatural singer
>   Like only those who know Him can.[3]

I say, "Tune your ear to the Supernatural." Sense His nearness—His powerful presence. Do whatever is necessary to march to His drumbeat. Start preparing yourself for New Testament Christianity. Put things in order for a mighty offensive of the Lord. Get ready for revival!

For Discussion and Reflection

1. What's the most recent memory you have of going to church on a Sunday morning with an expectation of encountering Christ?

2. Before reading this chapter, how would you have judged whether or not a given church was successful?

3. Does revival in the church sound like something good to you?

4. Revelation 3:20 is a strange picture of Christ knocking to gain entrance at the church door in the city of Laodicea. Put into modern terminology what will happen if the door is opened by someone.

5. Where is the North American church in the process of experiencing genuine revival? How far off is the "trigger point"?

Readings

DURING A SPIRITUAL AWAKENING, there is, first, an overwhelm ing awareness of the presence of God among His people.
"What have been the outstanding features of this move-ment?" asked Duncan Campbell of the Lewis revival in the years 1949–1953. "First, an awareness of God."[4] And then he went on to say, "I have no hesitation in saying that this awareness of God is the crying need of the Church today."[5]

—Ted S. Rendall, *Fire in the Church*, p. 19

"THIS LOVE FEAST at Fetter Lane [London, 739, during the Moravian Revival of the early 1700s] was a memorable one. Besides about sixty Moravians, there were present not fewer than seven of the Oxford Methodists, namely, John and Charles Wesley, George Whitefield, Wesley Hall, Benjamin Ingham, Charles Kinchin and Richards Hutchins, all of them ordained clergymen of the Church of England. Wesley writes: 'About three in the morning, as we were continuing instant in prayer, the power of God came mightily upon us, insomuch that many cried for exceeding joy, and many fell to the ground. As soon as we were recovered a little from that awe and amazement at the presence of His Majesty, we broke out with one voice—"We Praise Thee, O God; we acknowl-edge Thee to be the Lord!"'"

—Rev. John Greenfield, *When the Spirit Came: The Story of the Moravian Revival of 1727*, p. 35

MEN ARE ONLY MADE CONSCIOUS of God by the display of His attributes. They feel God when they sense His greatness, His love, or His wisdom. But in times of revival it is especially His power and His holiness that are in evidence. It is these that bring that deep conviction of sin among believing and unbelieving alike. In times of revival a man is not only made conscious that God is there, but often it will seem to him that He is there to deal with him alone. He becomes oblivious of everyone but himself in the agonising grip of a holy God. . . .

At times this strange sense of God may pervade a building, a community or a district, affecting those who come within its spell. In the Welsh Revival of 1904 near the town of Gorseinon a meeting continued throughout the night. A miner, a hardened godless character, returning from his shift about four A.M., saw the light in the chapel and decided to investigate. As soon as he opened the door he was overwhelmed by a sense of God's presence. He was heard to exclaim, "Oh, God is here!" He was afraid either to enter or depart, and there on the threshold of the chapel the work of salvation began in his heart. . . .

In the great American Revival of 1858, ships, as they drew near the American ports, seemed to come into a zone of the Spirit's influence. Ship after ship arrived with the same tale of sudden conviction and conversion. In one ship a captain and the entire crew of thirty men found Christ out at sea and entered the harbour rejoicing.

This sense of God bringing conviction of sin in its wake, is perhaps the outstanding feature of true revival. Not always is it the unconverted who are affected, as in the cases just quoted. Often it is believers, or those who profess to be, as in the revivals in Manchuria and China under Jonathan Goforth (1906–9), or in the more recent Congo Revival (1953). Describing the revival in Northampton, Mass.

(1735), Jonathan Edwards wrote, "The town seemed to be full of the presence of God. It never was so full of love, nor so full of joy, and yet so full of distress, as it was then." To cleansed hearts it is heaven, to convicted hearts hell, when God is in the midst.

—Arthur Wallis, *Revival: The Rain from Heaven*, pp. 49–51

— ◆ —

NEAR THE TIP of South India there resided the saintly Amy Carmichael, an Ulsterwoman from the County Down, whose mother and pastor had been 'impressed' in the great Ulster Revival of 1859. Amy Carmichael had devoted her life to the rescue of devadasis, little temple prostitutes, and around her mission house in Dohnavur had grown up a numerous Christian colony of workers, together with boy- and girl-orphans, children and teenagers. . . .

Amy Carmichael, in common with other folk in Tamilnad, had been praying with her helpers for a visitation of the Holy Spirit to all of India ever since the Welsh Revival and its overflow upon the Khasi Hills. Thus she wrote in her diary of events:

On October 22nd, to quote one of the little girls, Jesus came to Dohnavur. He was there before, but on that day He came in so vivid a fashion that we cannot wonder that it struck the child as a new Coming.

—J. Edwin Orr, *Evangelical Awakenings in Southern Asia*, p. 131

— ◆ —

. . . For 185 hours—without any interruption—the services [at Asbury College and Seminary, 1970] had continued! During all this time there was no pressure, no scheduled meetings, no paid advertising, no offering, no invocation, no prelude or postlude, and no benediction.

And no one tried to compile any statistics. It was felt that this would be out of keeping with the spirit of the revival. But most of the students on the campus of the college and seminary knelt at the altar, and there were thousands of other persons who made a similar dedication. The whole spiritual tone of the campus was completely changed.

The lights in Hughes Auditorium still have not been turned out. Even now, months later, a few people gather each evening to pray, witness, and rejoice together. Often these meetings last into the midnight hours, with visitors not infrequently being helped on to God. Also during most hours of the day someone may still be seen entering the chapel. They kneel to pray for a few minutes, then leave. Others just sit and stare at the altar so rife with precious memories. If one looks closely, tears may be seen coursing down their cheeks.

Perhaps those tears express more eloquently than words what has happened. There is no human vocabulary that can capture the full dimension of one divine moment. In some ways, it seems almost like a dream—yet it happened. We saw it with our eyes. In a way impossible to describe, God was in our midst. Those of us who were there can never look upon the things of this world quite the same.

—Howard Anke, Professor of Bible, Asbury College, writing in *One Divine Moment: The Asbury Revival*, edited by Robert E. Coleman, p. 25

GOD'S WORD SAYS that when we seek the Lord, He comes to His temple. We must check here to see what it is that we who are praying for revival are seeking. We are not seeking fame, miracles, success, ease, full churches, or financial deliverance. These *may* come. But first and foremost we seek the Lord. It is He who must come in power and glory.

—Leonard Ravenhill, *Revival Praying*, p. 147

2

Worship and Bow Down

— ◆ —

HUMAN BEINGS have a longing which I believe stretches as far back as the paradise of Eden. It's the desire to experience once again the wonder of the presence of the Lord.

This intimacy was first shown in the garden. But then Adam and Eve sinned and, the Bible records, instead of continuing to enjoy the divine closeness of their Lord, "The man and his wife hid themselves from the presence of God."

From that initial point, one can almost read Scripture as an account of repeated attempts by both the Creator and His creatures to restore the cherished relationship known at the start of human history.

This presence of the Lord is an important theme throughout the Old Testament. In Exodus 33:14, God promised Moses, "My Presence will go with you, and I will give you rest" (NIV). This divine promise was manifested supernaturally: "And the Lord went before them by day in a pillar of cloud to lead them along the way, and by night in a pillar of fire to give them light" (Exod. 13:21).

Recall as well how God's unique presence was known in the tabernacle ("Then the cloud covered the Tent of Meeting, and the glory of the Lord filled the tabernacle," Exod. 40:34, NIV) and later in the temple ("When Solomon finished praying, fire came down from heaven and consumed the burnt offering and the sacrifices, and the glory of the Lord filled the temple," 2 Chron. 7:1, NIV).

On a more personal level, the psalmist declared, "In thy presence is fulness of joy!" (Ps. 16:11). What a great truth is contained in David's simple statement! In another psalm he affirms what the prophet Jonah had to learn the hard way— that you can't easily flee from the presence of the Lord:

Whither shall I go from thy Spirit? Or whither shall I flee from thy presence? If I ascend to heaven, thou art there! If I make my bed in Sheol, thou art there! If I take the wings of the morning and dwell in the uttermost parts of the sea, even there thy hand shall lead me, and thy right hand shall hold me (Ps. 139:7-10).

But too often God's people, like Adam and Eve and Jonah, continued to hide and flee from the presence of the Lord. Or, more often, they simply grew indifferent to Him and continued their lives—even their religious lives—as if He were not really there.

Yet God, in His love, was preparing to make His presence known to His people in a far more personal way than He ever had before. As the prophets foretold, "The Lord whom you seek will suddenly come to his temple; the messenger of the covenant in whom you delight, behold, he is coming . . ." (Mal. 3:1). Or, more specifically, "Behold, a virgin shall conceive, and bear a son, and his name shall be called Emmanuel (which means God with us)"(Matt. 1:23, referring to Isa. 7:14).

In the New Testament, the Gospels record the fulfillment of these promises. Mary was told by the angel, "The Holy Spirit will come upon you, and the power of the Most High will overshadow you; therefore the child to be born will be called holy, the Son of God" (Luke 1:35). So the greatest of miracles happened when God took on flesh so human beings could know His presence firsthand.

When Christ ascended to glory, the church was next to know this divine presence through the Holy Spirit, who came at Pentecost and now empowers the church.

So the Lord's making His presence known to His own is not something new. Yet again, I fear that too often what the prophets wrote about their past generations seems to haunt this present one as well—God's people had eyes to see, but still didn't see Him all that well—and ears to hear, but just couldn't pick out His voice that clearly, either.

Unfortunately, this is even true today regarding many who regularly attend supposedly successful churches. If we are honest, we must admit that something important is missing, because this promised presence of the Lord isn't being experienced, and probably isn't even expected all that much.

And that's why I'm asking you, in this chapter and in those that follow, to imagine Christ is at your church in the flesh. Go back and picture Him once again, right there in your sanctuary.

What would happen if, on a given Sunday morning, the people in the congregation would suddenly have their eyes opened to the reality of Christ's presence, if they were to see the Lord sitting on the platform?

My feeling is that, before too long, numbers of people would quietly drop to their knees. Some might even stretch out prostrate before Christ.

Why? Because these body positions speak the universal language of worship. Even without words, such postures state the obvious . . . "You are worthy, Lord. I am only Your servant. But I do offer You my praise."

Awe, reverence, adoration, a holy fear, worship—all this is part of an immediate and natural response to our awareness of Christ's being present in His church. Its absence indicates that God's people have not developed the capacity to perceive Him as truly being present.

Now, back to our Sunday morning setting. Perhaps Jesus says, "Everyone please be seated and proceed with your service." How grateful you would be to have the choir sing the burgeoning expression of your inner self:

> God reveals His presence:
> Let us now adore Him,
> And with awe appear before Him.
> [Christ] is in His temple:
> All within keep silence,
> Prostrate lie with deepest reverence.
> Him alone
> God we own,
> Him our God and Saviour:
> Praise His Name for ever!

God reveals His presence:
Hear the harps resounding;
See the crowds the throne surrounding;
"Holy, holy, holy!"
Hear the hymn ascending,
Angels, saints, their voices blending.
Bow Thine ear
To us here;
Hearken, O Lord Jesus,
To our meaner praises.[1]

"How wonderful!" you would think. "The words are perfect. I must remember to say thank you to our music director and also to the choir members. Funny how I never appreciated all their work before. But as they were singing, I watched Jesus, and I believe their music truly ministered to Him."

With Christ bodily present, all the congregational hymns would take on new and powerful meaning. At times the words would almost seem to jump from the page:

All hail the power of Jesus' name!
Let angels prostrate fall;
Bring forth the royal diadem,
And crown Him Lord of all;
Bring forth the royal diadem,
And crown Him Lord of all!

O that with yonder sacred throng
We at His feet may fall!
We'll join the everlasting song,
And crown Him Lord of all;
We'll join the everlasting song,
And crown Him Lord of all![2]

When Christ is present, worship comes alive. Going to church is no longer just a self-centered act—to see what we'll get out of a service. Formality without meaning—just going through the motions—ceases. The "tradition" of singing hymns—words and melodies—without a companion inward expression vanishes. No, now it's full, heartfelt participation on our part.

Again, I remind you that our Lord *is* truly present in His church Sunday after Sunday. And what does that say about our worship practices?

This truth, when lived out, means that it is important not to arrive late. Tardiness is an affront. Lateness indicates a lax awareness—and how many of us are careless in this regard! If the President of the United States or the Queen of England were special guests in our churches, people would hurry to fill the closest pews. So why don't we do this when our Lord and Master is the honored guest?

People who are mature in worshiping the Lord train themselves to arrive at church fifteen to twenty minutes early. They can then read through the chosen hymns so they don't see the words for the first time as they're singing them. They can spend time in prayer, not asking that the Lord will be present—because He's already promised to be—but praying that the congregation might be keenly aware of the marvelous privilege afforded them.

Such early arrivers clear their minds of extraneous thoughts by purposely returning in their thinking to the cross. Mentally pausing at Calvary, or at the empty tomb, or at other scenes of their Lord's ministry as recorded in the Scriptures, they enhance their spiritual receptivity and prepare themselves to praise their Lord.

These eager worshipers could well have started getting ready for the Lord's Day on Saturday evening: their Bibles were read, they had a good night's sleep, and they were up in plenty of time with a keen sense of anticipation. They had a good breakfast so a growling stomach wouldn't distract them. They might have tucked a song about the Lord in their hearts to sing while getting ready.

Why all this preparation? Again, because these few hold a deep-seated conviction that Jesus will be present in His church when the congregation gathers, and they want to be ready to greet Him.

In fact, during times of genuine revival in the church, it is not uncommon for worshipers to begin gathering fifteen minutes or a half-hour—even forty-five minutes—early to pray in small groups or to begin singing praises to the Lord. When the sense of His presence is strong, worship is always a natural outgrowth.

The Presbyterian revivalist Charles Finney, ministering in the second quarter of the nineteenth century, pointed out that "during times of backsliding the truths of the Bible appear like a dream. Faith doesn't see God's truth standing out in bold relief in all the burning realities of eternity. But when a revival comes to the church, people no longer see men as trees walking."[3]

I affirm Finney's words. During revival, Christ's presence in His church is perceived in all its glorious truth. No, He is not physically present, but He's there nevertheless. And when Christ is recognized as being present, His people naturally, compellingly, take the time necessary to worship Him.

Some people think of worship as whatever takes place in the church when the congregation comes together: "We're going to worship." But I'm using the word more precisely. In essence, worship means *to attribute worth to God.*

In Scripture, worship occasionally refers to a broad response of God's people to the wonder of who He is. For example, in Romans 12:1, Paul writes, "I appeal to you therefore, brethren, by the mercies of God, to present your bodies as a living sacrifice, holy and acceptable to God, *which is your spiritual worship*" (emphasis added). But most frequently when the word is used in the Bible, it has to do with praising God—verbally attributing worth to Him.

Graham Kendrick in *Learning to Worship As a Way of Life* gives us additional helpful direction:

> It was an important discovery for me some years ago when I found out the full meaning of the original Greek word which is used most often in the New Testament and translated as

"worship." In fact, there are seven Greek words: five of these occur once, another occurs three times, but the final one appears no less than fifty-nine times. This word is *proskyneo*, and its overwhelming use compared to the other words must tell us something of its importance. The basic meaning is "to come towards to kiss (the hand)" and it denotes both the external act of prostrating oneself in worship and the corresponding inward attitude of reverence and humility.[4]

I fear that today most believers find worship of this sort to be a difficult activity. So perhaps it will be helpful to share an explanation of worship I used when my children were growing up. I would have them think of worship or adoration or praise as paying God a compliment, as though we were saying to the Lord, "I really like this about You"; and then telling Him exactly what we had in mind.

To do this well requires some forethought if we don't want our compliments to be meaningless. "Jesus, I like it that You are loving," my children would say. "Jesus, I'm glad there is nothing mean or bad about You." "Jesus, You don't tell lies." "Jesus, I want to tell You that I like it that You don't get tired and have to sleep."

I would ask my young ones, "Do you appreciate it when people say nice things about you?" Their reply, of course, was, "Yes!"

"And what if I got together a hundred people who all thought you were wonderful. And what if they would sing about how special you are. Would you enjoy that?"

"Yes! Yes!" they would chorus.

"Well, that's part of what we do for Christ in church on Sunday mornings. Sure, we go to hear what God will say to us as someone teaches us from His Word. But we also go to tell God how we feel about Him as His people. We sing His praises. We rehearse His good qualities by reviewing what the Scriptures say about Him or through someone's leading us in a prayer of praise. Understand?"

"Now," I would continue, "if we don't believe Jesus is there to hear us, that's no fun, is it? But is He there to hear us, even if we can't see Him?"

"Yes, yes! He's there!"

"Oh, come on, now. How can Jesus be there if we can't see Him?"

"By His Spirit."

"But do you really believe that?"

"Yes! Yes!"

"Are you sure?"

In childlike simplicity, they would affirm this profound truth so central to Scripture, the very one most grownups miss. How sad, because when as adults we actually no longer believe in the reality of the divine presence, this lack of belief will affect how we sing the songs, how we hear the Scriptures read, and how we listen to the choir. I pray that my children will never forget, will never grow habitual in this negligence.

"Tell me," I would ask them. "Which is better? To have a record attendance at church, or to have Jesus present with us?"

"To have Jesus present."

"But what about this: Is it better to have a brand-new church building, or to have Jesus present with us?"

"To have Jesus present."

"Well now, which is better—to have the mayor come, and the district superintendent of the denomination, and a famous Christian athlete—all on the same morning—or to have Jesus present?"

"To have Jesus!"

And they were right—because nothing, absolutely nothing, matches the privilege of experiencing anew the delightful presence of our Lord in church on Sunday morning. How can a church be considered successful if this kind of awareness is absent? And what better way to respond to this truth than through the expression of heartfelt worship, adoration, praise—the first measurement of revival?

"When Christ Came to Church" is a chapter title in Dr. V. Raymond Edman's book, *Out of My Life*. Doc Edman was president at Wheaton College when I was a student there. Although he is with the Lord now, he still speaks to me through his writings. This particular chapter retells the life-changing experience of Dr. A. J. Gordon, the Baptist preacher of late nineteenth-century Boston after whom Gordon College and Gordon-Conwell Seminary in Massachusetts are named. An extended section from Edman's book captures exactly what I have been saying:

It was Saturday night when wearied from the work of preparing Sunday's sermon, I fell asleep and the dream came. I was in the pulpit just ready to begin my sermon when a stranger entered and passed slowly up the left aisle of the church. He proceeded nearly halfway up the aisle when a gentleman stepped out and offered him a place in his pew, which was quietly accepted.

Excepting the face and features of the stranger, everything in the scene is distinctly remembered. Only the countenance of the visitor could never be recalled. But as I began my sermon, my attention became riveted on this hearer. If I would avert my eyes from him for a moment, they would instinctively return to him, so that he held my attention rather than I held his till the discourse ended.

After the benediction the departing congregation filed into the aisles, but before I could reach him, the visitor had left the house. The one with whom he sat remained, however, and approaching him with great eagerness I asked, "Can you tell me who that stranger was who sat in your pew this morning?"

In the most matter-of-fact way he replied, "Why do you not know that man? It was Jesus of Nazareth!" With a sense of keenest disappointment I said, "My dear sir, why did you let him go without introducing him to me?"

With the same nonchalant air, the gentleman replied, "Oh, don't be troubled. He has been here today, and no doubt he will come again."

And now came an indescribable rush of emotion. The Lord himself, whose I am and whom I serve, has been listening to me today. What was I saying? Was I preaching on some popular theme in order to catch the ear of the public? Was he impressed with the music and the order of worship?

It didn't seem at that moment as though I could ever again care or have the smallest curiosity as to what men might say of preaching, worship or church if I could only know that he had not been displeased, that he would not withhold his feet from coming again because he had been grieved at what He might have seen or heard.

One thing lingered in my mind with something of comfort and more of awe. *He has been here today and no doubt he will come again.* [5]

Edman writes that for God's servant the dream encounter was "a momentous occasion." The Lord Jesus had been listening to [Gordon's] preaching, and he had not known that he who was there was the one who could best evaluate his ministry. The impact of that immediacy of the Lord's presence transformed A. J. Gordon's ministry and that of many others through his life and testimony. Thereafter, his life was marked by two compelling realities—he is here today, and he will come again! [6]

It seems to me this is the great missing truth of the North American church: Christ is here today, and He will come again! We need to recapture this truth, to reclaim our heritage as the people to whom God reveals Himself—to know a spiritual regenesis.

Few in churches are preachers like A. J. Gordon, but all are potential worshipers. Christ is here today, and He will come again! Can we not do our part each Sunday to attribute to Christ the glory due His name?

I personally believe the Lord has been preparing His church to be able to express its praise to Him in a new and exciting way. In the last ten to fifteen years, a whole new music of congregational praise has come into being. This is a worship music that people can sing spontaneously: "Father, I adore you"; "Worthy is the Lamb who was slain"; "Alleluia"; "Surely, the presence of the Lord is in this place" . . . and on and on.

Times of revival (or again, those times in the church marked by an overwhelming sense of Christ's presence) are classically accompanied by new and significant hymnody which allows the people to verbalize in song their rediscovery of the Presence. Before the Reformation, congregations listened passively to the great music of the organ and the complicated polyphonic singing of trained choirs, but the reformers found words to be sung in common vernacular. Huss, Luther, the Moravians all encouraged congregational singing.

In fact, many of our favorite hymn writers wrote in response to the effect of revivalist movements on their own spiritual condition. Paul Gerhardt of Germany, Count von Zinzendorf, Isaac Watts, the Welsh William Williams, the Irish Augustus Toplady—all created songs a people could sing ("O Sacred Head, Now Wounded," "Joy to the World," "Guide Me, O Thou Great Jehovah," "Rock of Ages," and more). Charles Wesley helped turn England upside down spiritually, and he is also credited with over six thousand hymns. He often used folk songs, opera melodies, and bar tunes, as well as familiar lines from psalters to create such hymn standards as "Rejoice, the Lord Is King" and "O For a Thousand Tongues to Sing." All these hymnodists and others such as John Newton and William Cowper put songs in the souls of men and women so that the truths of revival movements were indelibly imprinted through refrains and stanzas and choruses among a singing people.

Our modern new worship music, coupled with these great traditional hymns of the church, has equipped God's people to be able to praise Christ today in a way they couldn't have some years before. How wonderful! I believe this singing is one of the vital signs that God is preparing His people for a great new work of His Spirit.

When that comes, it won't matter whether we meet in a sanctuary or in a gymnasium; whether fifty are present or five hundred; whether the people are from the inner city or from the most exclusive of suburbs; whether they are Baptist, Lutheran, Presbyterian, or Nazarene. If all present are encountering the risen Christ and offering to Him their praise, He will be most pleased.

And suddenly the church of God will become exciting. We will be in the midst of renewal, of spiritual regenesis. And the longing of God's people will finally be fulfilled as we are able to declare with conviction, "He has been here today, and no doubt He will come again!"

For Discussion and Reflection

1. Why is a renewed interest in worship often an early sign of revival?

2. Has the lesson of A. J. Gordon's dream marked your life yet? When is Christ most likely to next visit the church where you attend? Anticipating that event, in what ways can you prepare yourself to be ready to worship Him?

3. Do you have any constructive suggestions as to how the Sunday morning service at your church can be made more worshipful?

4. What are the advantages and disadvantages of Christ's *bodily* being a part of your congregation?

5. Worship doesn't have to be limited to church on Sunday. Take some time today to write down ten carefully chosen qualities you like about Christ. Read your list to Him tonight when you pray.

Readings

ANOTHER RESULT of the revival [Shantung, China, 1932–33] was a continual singing of the people. They put songs and other scriptures to music. Old people who could not read or write memorized the songs and sang with their eyes closed, their bodies swaying to the rhythm of the melody and tears of joy running down their cheeks. God had taken away their sorrow and given them a new song. I saw that many old women who could not carry a tune were filled with the Spirit, singing a melody that seemed to come from an angel of heaven.

One of the greatest personal blessings which I received from the revival was the wonderful spirit in the worship services. Entire congregations bowed in silent meditation for several minutes, and the atmosphere became charged with spiritual power. Suddenly someone would begin to pray and praise God. As long as an hour would pass before the speaker could speak. Conviction became so evident that the preacher would simply give an opportunity for anyone who wished to accept Christ to come forward, and there was always some response, often large groups. I knew it was the natural result of a spirit of worship and adoration which followed revival.

The ordinances also became more meaningful. One missionary commented, "I was never so blessed in my life as when taking the Lord's Supper with Spirit-filled Chinese brothers and sisters in Christ."

It was not unusual to see people in tears during the observance. As one young widow told a missionary, "My eyes were streaming tears all the time. It wasn't that I was sad or glad; it was simply that I was broken before the Lord."

Baptism took on new meaning. Unbelievers, witnessing the baptisms, often came under deep conviction. Invitations were frequently given and conversions resulted. I realized I had never fully understood the meaning of worship until I saw the Spirit of God renewing the hearts of His people.

—C. L. Culpepper, *The Shantung Revival*, pp. 66–67

— ◆ —

I BELIEVE we ought to have again the old Biblical concept of God which makes God awful and makes men lie face down and cry, "Holy, holy, holy, Lord God Almighty." That would do more for the church than everything or anything else.

Then there is *admiration*, that is, appreciation of the excellency of God. Man is better qualified to appreciate God than any other creature because he was made in His image and is the only creature who was. This admiration for God grows and grows until it fills our heart with wonder and delight. "In our astonished reverence we confess Thine uncreated loveliness," said the hymn writer. "In our astonished reverence." The God of the modern evangelical rarely astonishes anybody. He manages to stay pretty much within the constitution. Never breaks over our bylaws. He's a very well-behaved God and very denominational and very much one of us, and we ask Him to help us when we're in trouble and look to Him to watch over us when we're asleep. The God of the modern evangelical isn't a God I could have much respect for. But when the Holy Ghost shows us God as He is we admire Him to the point of wonder and delight.

—A. W. Tozer, *Worship: The Missing Jewel of the Evangelical Church*, pp. 26–27

— ◆ —

[A FIRST-HAND ACCOUNT of the Welsh Revival of 1904–1905:] Everything sprang into new life. Former blasphemers were the most eloquent, both in prayer and praise. These men appeared to be making up for lost time—"the years that the locust hath eaten" (Joel 2:25). Drunkards forgot the way to the saloons, which in fact were empty in a few nights. All the former inebriates were busy worshiping. Scores of the most respectable young people of the churches, who had previously never entertained such a thought, joined together and preached in the common, where gypsies usually camped. There they showed the benighted ones the simple way of salvation. Nothing daunted or discouraged them. Was it not the "new wine" of the kingdom that made them bold and merry of heart? It was the young people who responded with greatest alacrity to the searching challenge of absolute surrender and consecration to the service of the Lord. Wherever they went, the very air became vibrant with songs of praise. Hundreds of them, thrilled with an experience to which they had hitherto been strangers, scattered the "divine flame" recklessly abroad—to be seen once in a lifetime! But it was a wonderful privilege to have witnessed, at least once, a land in the throes of revival.

—David Matthews, *I Saw the Welsh Revival*, p. 23

THOSE COMPETENT TO JUDGE have affirmed that the root meaning of the Hebrew word [for *worship*] carries the thought of "a dog to its master." . . .

Let us use an illustration to clarify this point. We will suppose that a man, warmly clad, ventures forth on a blustery and bitterly cold night. The temperature is below zero, and the streets are practically deserted. Presently he sees a poor, neglected, shivering and half starved cur, sheltering behind a telephone pole from the biting wind. Some cruel boys have tied a can to its tail, and it has been kicked from pillar to post, until now it is almost at the end of its tether. It will never survive a night like this on the streets.

The man pauses and looks the dog over. What a pitiable sight it is: thin, miserable, frightened, homeless, hungry and on its last legs! His compassion is stirred and, yielding to the impulse of the moment, he stoops down, reaches out his hand and calls to the dog. Suspicious at first, for the dog has good reasons for distrusting mankind, it gradually approaches, until at length it comes under his hand. The man pats it on the head, strokes it, all the while speaking kindly words. Then, after removing the string and the can from its tail, he lifts it up, opens his overcoat, pops it in, and carries it back to his home. When he enters his home he says to his wife: "I've found a poor starving dog on the street, that will surely die tonight, unless it finds a home. Please put a sack in the corner of the kitchen and we'll take care of it for at least tonight." Accordingly, the dog is gently placed on the sack, and a delicious bowl of hot bread and milk is given it, followed by some scraps from the evening meal. For the first time in many days the dog wags its tail in gratitude for this unusual kindness.

The next morning it greets its benefactors with another friendly wag of its tail, and they decide to give it a permanent home. A month passes by, and what a wonderful change it produces in that dog! As a result of good food and proper care, one would scarcely recognize the fine looking animal as that miserable starving cur of four weeks ago.

One evening, as the man is sitting in an easy chair, with one hand hanging over the arm of the chair, he suddenly feels something warm and wet on his hand. Glancing down he sees the dog looking up at him with adoring eyes as, again and again, it licks the hand of the one to whom it owes everything. The dog had not come into the room to beg for a bone, or even to be petted. It wanted nothing from its owner but the privilege of sitting in his presence, so that it might look at him with rapt, adoring eyes and, every now and then, to enjoy the privilege of licking the hand of the one whom it loved above all others. This is *worship*.

—A. P. Gibbs, *Worship: The Christian's Highest Occupation*, pp. 62–64

— ◆ —

IN THE FIRST MONTH of the first year of his reign, [King Hezekiah] opened the doors of the temple of the Lord and repaired them. He brought in the priests and the Levites, assembled them . . . and said. . . . "Now I intend to make a covenant with the Lord, the God of Israel, so that his fierce anger will turn away from us. My sons, do not be negligent now, for the Lord has chosen you to stand before him and serve him, to minister before him and to burn incense." . .

When they had assembled . . . and consecrated themselves, they went in to purify the temple of the Lord, as the king had ordered, following the word of the Lord. The priests went into the sanctuary of the Lord to purify it. They brought out to the courtyard of the Lord's temple everything unclean that they found in the temple of the Lord. The Levites took it and carried it out to the Kidron Valley. They began the consecration on the first day of the first month, and by the eighth day of the month they reached the portico of the Lord. For eight more days they consecrated the temple of the Lord itself, finishing on the sixteenth day of the first month. . . .

Hezekiah gave the order to sacrifice the burnt offering on the altar. As the offering began, singing to the Lord began also, accompanied by trumpets and the instruments of David king of Israel. The whole assembly bowed in worship, while the singers sang and the trumpeters played. All this continued until the sacrifice of the burnt offering was completed.

When the offerings were finished, the king and everyone present with him knelt down and worshiped. King Hezekiah and his officials ordered the Levites to praise the Lord with the words of David and of Asaph the seer. So they sang praise with gladness and bowed their heads and worshiped. . . .

So the service of the temple of the Lord was reestablished. Hezekiah and all the people rejoiced at what God had brought about for his people, because it was done so quickly.

—2 Chronicles 29:3–36, NIV

3

They'll Know Us
By Our Love

— ◆ —

GIVEN THE OPTION, I presume most people would superficially assent to the idea of Christ's being a part of their church. But would they actually agree to the profound changes His presence would impose upon a congregation?

Say Jesus chose to make His presence known not only in spirit, but in the flesh, and He actually applied for membership in your local body. He's not going to usurp the pulpit or take over the chairperson role on all boards and committees. But He will offer to help others fill these roles (as He always has), except now you'll be able to see and hear and touch Him.

Frankly, having Christ bodily present, even playing a behind-the-scenes role, would significantly alter the spiritual life of most local churches, challenging many of us with lifestyle changes that might raise strong resistance on our part.

We have already said that if Christ were seen on Sundays during the morning service, the worship would come alive; adoration, praise, and exaltation would take on a whole new dimension during that hour together.

Let me now add a second element characteristic of having Jesus present in church. When Christ is active in a given congregation, it's not going to be long before people start hearing His insistence that there be love in the body, that His people begin exercising compassion for one another.

Insistence probably isn't a strong enough word, but I'm hesitant to utilize our Lord's terminology from Scripture—*command*—because a good way to empty a church quickly is to just issue a command or two.

For instance, if a pastor rashly said anything from the pulpit like, "The following is not a suggestion; I'm issuing a *command.* You are all to arrive on time for worship. Latecomers will no longer be seated or allowed to attend the service!

Again, this is a *command* you are expected to obey. From now on, come on time!"

This autocratic approach would send out a few fast ripples, wouldn't it?

Or how about the following announcement: "In an effort to balance our books, your board of trustees now *commands* all members of this parish to contribute 12 percent of your gross income to the church's general fund. Lack of compliance with this order will result in disciplinary action"? Or how about this: "All high school students at First Church are *commanded* to attend your youth group next Sunday night. Let me repeat, this is a *command*"?

Most of us take instant umbrage when we feel we are being pushed around. So now you know why I'm hesitant to remind you that Christ said, "This I *command* you, to love one another." Though this particular Scripture quote is taken from John 15 (v. 17, emphasis added), Christ's command for us to love is found often in John's writings: "And this commandment we have from him, that he who loves God should love his brother also" (1 John 4:21); "A new commandment I give to you, that you love one another" (John 13:34); "And this is his commandment, that we should . . . love one another, just as he has commanded us" (1 John 3:23); "This is my commandment, that you love one another *as I have loved you*" (John 15:12, emphasis added).

So consequently, in order to eliminate the resistance we normally feel toward authoritarian commands, let me simply state: the privilege of having the Lord Jesus Christ with us in the church carries with it His *insistence* that we love one another.

This means that if a church wants Jesus to make His presence consistently known, its people have to place a moratorium on sins such as gossip and carrying grudges, on closing their hearts to others' needs, on forming exclusive little cliques, on snooty superiority feelings—the list can get pretty long. All these love negatives have to be eliminated because when Christ is being welcomed to His church, He commands—well, He insists—on our loving one another.

That's why the church can't tolerate bigotry within its ranks. Her people must not develop a proficiency in verbal putdowns. Injurious humor must be carefully avoided. Christians dare not be two-faced in their friendships. Any attitude or action that smacks of disrespect for each other has to stop—at the command of the King!

What must reign in Christ's church is love. His people must master treating others the way their Lord does, always seeking the best for the other (a good definition of Christlike love).

Love is not the same as syrupy sentimentalism or nicey-nice surface talk. Sometimes Christlike love means saying the hard thing to someone because it's the truthful and, in the end result, the most loving thing to do. Even tough love, however, must bear the imprint of Christlikeness. It must be patient and kind, not rude or irritable. First Corinthians 13 becomes the model for this human mirror of divine love: "Love is not jealous or boastful; It . . . does not insist on its own way . . . it does not rejoice at wrong, but rejoices in the right. Love bears all things, believes all things, hopes all things, endures all things" (vv. 4–7).

Were you aware that high-water times in the church are always marked by the demonstration of unusual degrees of Christian love? The Scriptures record that in the early church the company of those who believed was of *one* heart (Acts 4:32). They lovingly shared what was theirs with those in the church who had needs. Why? They remembered that Jesus had recently taught, "By this all men will know that you are my disciples, if you have love for one another" (John 13:35).

Spreading the gospel for these first-century believers was important, but as one of their most influential teachers stressed, "If I speak in the tongues of men and of angels, but have not love, I am a noisy gong or a clanging cymbal. And if I have prophetic powers, and understand all mysteries and all knowledge, and if I have all faith, so as to remove mountains, but have not love, I am nothing. If I give away all I have, and if I deliver my body to be burned, but have not love, I gain nothing" (1 Corinthians 13:1–3).

Strong words, aren't they? One begins to suspect that Christ's standard of judging success in the church is at drastic variance with our own:

"But Lord, just listen to the sound of our marvelous new organ!"

"Our faith promises for missions have increased six years in a row."

"Last Easter our pageant was so good it got a half-page spread in the newspaper, including several pictures. And *they* even called *us* this year, wanting to send out a reporter again."

"Not only does our pastor have two earned doctorates, he's written six books—what's that You ask, Jesus? You want to know if our people love each other? Well, uh—sometimes that's hard to evaluate, isn't it? Can something as intangible as love in the body be measured?

"What's that You want to know, Lord?—Any people who aren't talking to each other? Any teens in the high school group who are shunned by the more popular kids? Any elderly folk who feel forgotten? Any singles who struggle, not really sensing they belong to our church family? Any widows needing someone to cry with a few more times yet? Any folk needing food or clothes or a little spending money?

"Well, Lord, I certainly hope not. We'll have to check things out with the youth leaders. You know, it's hard to get all these needs to surface. Our morning service isn't structured that much for sharing—Uh, what's that? Any people who have come to our church burdened down by sin, needing someone to put a loving spiritual arm around them and share about how the Father in heaven longs for His prodigal children to return to Him? . . ."

I don't really need to go on. I think it's clear that if many of us were in dialogue with Christ regarding standards for a successful church, we might be forced to begin radical reevaluations about the way we treat one another.

("What was I saying about the organ?—later, it can wait! That woman in the back pew looks lonely . . .")

The story of David Brainerd gives a beautiful picture of what it's like when a people sense Christ's presence and in turn begin loving one another.

Brainerd was a missionary to the Indians during what is called the Great Awakening, that memorable outpouring of the Holy Spirit on colonial America that took place during the 1730s and 40s. This young man, who was engaged to the daughter of the great preacher Jonathan Edwards, brought many Indians to Christ before he died of tuberculosis at age twenty-nine, having contracted the same disease which so ravaged the American tribes.

In the book, *Valiant for the Truth,* David Otis Fuller gives us a taste of Brainerd's ministry:

> Wilderness hardships, lack of proper food, overwork, and a consuming passion to win as many for Christ as possible in his lifetime drained Brainerd's meager physical resources. He was never a well man, even as a youth, and his diary is full of pathetic jottings on the subject: "I felt my bodily strength fail" . . . or "Shattered with the violence of the fever."[1]

The following excerpt from Brainerd's actual diary (which he never intended to be published) is dated 22 November 1744:

> At night I lost my way in the wilderness and wandered over mountains, through swamps, and most dangerous places. I was greatly exposed, much pinched with cold, with sickness at my stomach, so that every step was distressing to me.
>
> Thus I have frequently lain out the whole night, but God has preserved me. Such hardships serve to wean me from the earth, and will make heaven the sweeter.[2]

Oswald Smith writes that 1745 was the year of the Great Awakening among Brainerd's Indians:

> After suffering as few have suffered, after toiling day and night, after countless hours spent in praying and fasting, after

preaching and testifying in season and out, at last the break came, the fire fell.[3]

Brainerd's journal dated 6 August 1745 reads:

[The Indians] seemed eager of hearing; but there appeared nothing very remarkable, except their attention, till near the close of the discourse; and then Divine truths were attended with a surprising influence. There were scarcely three in forty who could refrain from tears and bitter cries.

They all as one seemed in an agony of soul to obtain an interest in Christ. . . . It was surprising to see how their hearts seemed to be pierced with the tender and melting invitations of the gospel, where there was not a word of terror spoken to them. . . .

So surprising were now the doings of the Lord, that I can say no less of this day, and I need say no more of it, than that the arm of the Lord was powerfully and marvelously revealed in it.[4]

What Brainerd is reporting here, of course, is that unmistakable sign of revival, an overwhelming sense of the presence of the Lord.

The next two days:

August 7. . . . Many [are] in great distress for their souls; and some few could neither go nor stand, but lay flat on the ground as if pierced at heart, crying incessantly for mercy. . . . It was remarkable that, as fast as they came from remote places round about, the Spirit of God seemed to seize them with concern for their souls. . . .

August 8. . . . I stood amazed at the influence, which seized the audience most universally; and could compare it to nothing more aptly than the irresistible force of a mighty torrent, or a swelling deluge, that with its unsupportable weight and pressure bears down and sweeps before it whatever comes in its way.[5]

This language—"a mighty torrent that sweeps before it whatever comes in its way"—is typical of revival reports. One can read descriptions like this in revival accounts that vary widely in terms of time and place, culture and personalities.

Brainerd again:

> They were almost universally praying and crying for mercy.
> . . . Numbers could neither go nor stand. Their concern was so
> great . . . that none seemed to take any notice of those about
> them, but each prayed freely for himself. . . .
> August 9. While I was discoursing near night a Divine influ-
> ence seemed to attend what was spoken in a powerful manner.[6]

Notice again that terminology so common to revival descriptions: "a Divine influence," which is the overwhelming presence of Christ through His Spirit.

> It was very affecting to see the poor Indians, who the other
> day were hallooing and yelling in their idolatrous feasts and
> drunken frolics, now crying to God with such importunity for
> an interest in His dear Son![7]

Now, finally, the record of August 25, the Lord's Day, just
a little over two weeks later:

> Love seemed to reign among them! They took each other by
> the hand with tenderness and affection, as if their hearts were
> knit together, while I was discoursing to them; and all their
> deportment towards each other was such, that a serious specta-
> tor might justly be excited to cry out with admiration, "Behold
> how they love one another!"
> Numbers of the other Indians, on seeing and hearing these
> things, were much affected, and wept bitterly; longing to be
> partakers of the same joy and comfort, which these discovered
> by their very countenances, as well as by their conduct.[8]

What a fabulous account of the effect of the "Divine influence"! Little wonder that John Wesley gave this advice: "Let
every preacher read carefully the life of David Brainerd."
K. Neill Foster is a man with a much more current testimony. In his book, *A Revolution of Love,* he tells about the
Western Canadian revivals in the 1970s:

Suddenly something broke. Perhaps it was our Anglo-Saxon reserve giving way before the unction of the Holy Spirit. Though words are inadequate, there was an explosion of love. It seemed as if the campgrounds were covered with love. And who is to say they were not? Hundreds of witnesses would agree: you could "feel" it. And when revival later came to Saskatoon, we had no trouble understanding our brethren when they said, "We are wading knee-deep in love."[9]

I believe it's fair to state that in *all* accounts of genuine revival, or whenever there's this overwhelming sense of the Lord's presence, you will inevitably read about or witness people who passionately love each other with Christlike love.

As the contemporary chorus states,

And they'll know we are Christians by our love, by our love,
And they'll know we are Christians by our love.

Despite how Christ's command pinches our chosen petty discriminations, our insidious prejudices, our hateful attitudes and actions, a loving community in an unloving world is still incredibly attractive—and a telltale sign that His presence is felt among us.

Do God's people through North America want to experience afresh the privilege of sensing the risen Christ in their churches? I'm often asked this question, and my answer is: I believe they do. My conviction is that, if surveyed, Christians will place the continued realization of Christ's presence as a priority above matters like a new sanctuary or gym, an additional couple of staff members, an increase in giving, or a dynamic youth or senior adult program. Given a choice, they will opt for the coming of Christ anew to His church any day.

But do Christians realize that when their Lord is present He will insist on them loving one another? This reality needs to penetrate our souls.

Revival can come in different ways. Where there has been widespread backsliding, this infusion of new life usually

begins with a deep conviction of sin, which leads to repentance or a dramatic change of direction. But for maturing believers who want to know Christ more, revival can start with
a new understanding of His insistence that His followers
truly love one another, which the Lord then honors with
greater and greater manifestations of His presence.

We can pray for the ability to love one another more, to be
obedient to what we see in Scripture, to act out our new
intents, to confess where we fail, then to watch as we receive
more and more love as well as an intensified and growing
awareness of Christ with us.

So I challenge us to continue to pray for a deep Spirit of
conviction in the church, for rapt attention and tears in our
services when God's Word is preached. But I call as well for
greater obedience even now in this area of learning to love
one another as Christ Himself modeled and insisted upon—
indeed, commanded!

For Discussion and Reflection

1. Do you believe Christ intentionally used the word "command" when He said that His people were to love one another? Explain your answer.

2. On a scale of one to ten, ten being the best, rate your church as to how well it is obeying Christ's command that we love one another.

3. If everybody in your church expressed Christian love the same way you do, would the ratings go up or down? Why?

4. Why does a lack of genuine love in a church make it harder for people to sense the presence of Christ?

5. Who best exemplifies the love of Christ in your church? What questions would you ask this individual if you talked together?

Readings

ON FEBRUARY 22, 1970, a spontaneous revival broke out in Anderson, Indiana, an industrial city of 75,000, and went unabated for fifty consecutive days. . . . On that eventful day, a group of students from Asbury College came to the South Meridian Church of God to share what had taken place on that campus on February 3, 1970. As these seven students shared what Christ had done in their lives, the Holy Spirit descended upon this expectant and hungry people. . . .

The most powerful emotion of the entire meeting was *love.* The meeting was called "The Revival of Love." It was not a sentimental, "sticky" type of love; it was the pure love of God as described in First Corinthians 13. It was something one could "feel," and it drew people to Christ and to each other. Husbands and wives were reconciled, fathers and sons prayed together, the generation gap was bridged, and the racial barrier was lifted. . . .

This was the quality of the love we experienced during the revival—no one was outside or beyond the scope of God's love, regardless of age, culture, religion, or race.

—Charles R. Tarr, *A New Wind Blowing,* pp. 11, 15–16

PRAYER

LET THY unwearied and tender love to me
make my love unwearied and tender to my neighbor,
zealous to pray for and to procure and promote
his health and safety, ease and happiness.

Make me peaceable and reconcilable, easy to forgive,
and glad to return good for evil.

Amen.

—John Wesley, in *Devotions and Prayers of John Wesley,*
edited by Donald E. Demaray, pp. 26–27

— ◆ —

LOVE EXPLODES in the congregation!
It is convulsed by the Holy Spirit!
This is the revolution of love!
These are strange new terms in the Christian vocabulary.
Let us attempt an explanation of them by illustration.

In June of 1972 a revival team visited the Labason Evangelical Church on the Island of Mindanao, Republic of the
Philippines. The telegram we had sent to announce our
coming had not arrived. Besides, the Vacation Bible School
was in progress.

But never mind, there would be a service, the pastor decided. The building itself was ample in size but unfinished. A
dirt floor. Cement blocks for a platform and altar. Open windows. Lanterns in the evening. Still, on brief notice, the people came. And their hearts were hungry.

The revival team shared, each relating with deep honesty
just how the Holy Spirit had dealt with him. An invitation
was given.

Many of the believers moved forward to the altar, some
began to weep, confessions were made to God and one another and Christian love began to be expressed.

Words fail, but a kind of divine epidemic had been unleashed. A holy convulsion was cleansing the church.

Remarkably enough, in a second service in the same
church a few days later, there was a further purging and if
possible, a greater outpouring of love.

Undeniable revival.
Transparent honesty.
And love, such love.

The theme song of the revival team that visited Labason was strikingly appropriate. Composed earlier by the Daniebelle singers during a World Vision evangelistic crusade in Zamboanga, its lilting melody and powerful words proved a catalyst for revival wherever the teams went, first in Mindanao and later in the island of Luzon.

> Oh, there's a revolution of love in Labason,
> You can feel the Spirit moving in the air,
> There's a revolution of love in Labason
> See the smiling happy faces everywhere.
> Oh, I love you, my brother and my sister,
> If you listen you can hear the people say:
> There's a revolution of love in Labason
> And you can join the revolution today.

> —K. Neill Foster, *A Revolution of Love*, pp. 13–14

— ◆ —

A *SPIRIT OF UNCHARITABLENESS* is evidence of a backslidden heart. By this, I mean a want of that disposition that puts the best construction upon every one's conduct that can be reasonable—a want of confidence in the good intentions and professions of others. We naturally credit the good professions of those whom we love. We naturally attribute to them right motives, and put the best allowable construction upon their words and deeds. Where there is a want of this there is evidence conclusive of a backslidden or unloving heart.

A *censorious spirit* is conclusive evidence of a backslidden heart. This is a spirit of fault-finding, of impugning the motives of others, when their conduct admits of a charitable construction. It is a disposition to fasten blame upon others, and judge them harshly. It is a spirit of distrust of Christian character and profession. It is a state of mind that reveals itself in harsh judgments, harsh sayings, and the manifestation of uncomfortable feelings toward individuals. This state of mind is entirely incompatible with a loving heart, and whenever a censorious spirit is manifested by [one who professes] religion, you may know there is a backslidden heart.

—Charles Finney, *Revival Lectures*, p. 493

REV. B. W. STONE, a Presbyterian minister in Bourbon County, Kentucky, hearing of the wonderful works of God in Logan County, traveled across the state early in 1801 to see for himself what God had wrought. Upon his return to his own parish, his account of the things he had seen and heard made such a powerful impression upon his people that within a few weeks a similar revival broke out in that field, at Cane Ridge, which became one of the influential awakenings in this whole period.

Writing of the events of those days, Mr. Stone relates: "A memorable meeting was held at Cane Ridge in August, 1801. The roads were crowded with wagons, carriages, horses and footmen moving to the solemn camp. It was judged that between twenty and thirty thousand persons were assembled. Four or five preachers spoke at the same time in different parts of the encampment without confusion. The Methodist and Baptist preachers aided in the work, and all appeared cordially united in it. They were of one mind and soul. . . . We all engaged in singing the same songs, all united in prayer, all preached the same gospel. The numbers converted will be known only in eternity. Many things transpired in the meeting which were so much like miracles that they had the same effect as miracles on unbelievers. By them many were convinced that Jesus was the Christ, and were persuaded to submit to Him. This meeting continued six or seven days and nights, and would have continued longer, but food for such a multitude failed. To this meeting many had come from Ohio and other distant parts. These returned home and diffused the same spirit in their respective neighborhoods, and similar results followed."

—Fred W. Hoffman, *Revival Times in America*, pp. 76–77

4

Walking in the Light

— ◆ —

WE HUMANS LONG for more of God's presence.

But without a doubt, Christ also yearns for close fellowship with the people in His church. He doesn't want to be perceived as far removed from believers who join together in His name. He wants us by faith to sense His presence.

Hasn't Christ promised that when even two or three gather in His name He will be in their midst? This promise certainly indicates our Lord's desire that His presence be not only understood, but appreciated and experienced.

Even the spiritually lukewarm congregation at Laodicea in Revelation 3 was told by Christ, "I stand at the door and knock." What an incredible picture!—our Lord knocking, knocking at the door of His church, wanting in, wanting His presence to be recognized, wanting to be welcomed.

Why does He humble himself to beg our invitation?

"If any one hears My voice and opens the door," Christ says, "I will come in to him and eat with him, and he with Me." In other words,"I want someone in the church to welcome Me so we can enjoy close fellowship, so that you can experience this truth that I am literally with you."

The apostle John begins his first Epistle with this same emphasis—the delight of fellowship with Christ in His church: "That which we have seen and heard [regarding Christ] we proclaim also to you, so that you may have fellowship with us; and our fellowship is with the Father and with his Son Jesus Christ" (1 John 1:3).

But then John continues in a different vein: "If we say we have fellowship with him while we walk in darkness, we lie and do not live according to the truth, but if we walk in the light, as he is in the light, we have fellowship with one another, and the blood of Jesus his Son cleanses us from all sin" (vv. 6–7).

In other words, John is saying that to experience this

ongoing fellowship with Christ in His church, His people need to walk in the light. Fellowship with God and Jesus is antithetical to the walk of His people in sin-filled shadows, to their slipping in and out of half-light or deliberately stepping onto dark paths.

Or, as 1 John 2:6 states, "He who says he abides in him [which is another way of talking about being close to Christ] ought to walk in the same way in which he [Jesus] walked."

Now, let's go back to the question I've been asking all along: What would it be like if Christ physically took an active role in our churches? Again, we know that, by His Spirit, Christ *is* literally with us whenever His body congregates; yet we need to work at visualizing this great truth of His nearness. So let's again think of our Lord as also being a part of the fellowship at your church.

We have already established that adoration would be an immediate and natural response to a startling awareness of Christ's presence. We would also be acutely aware of His insistence on our loving one another. Now, let me add another thought: To experience *ongoing* fellowship with Christ in His church, His people must walk in the light. Restated, they must learn to live consistently in a spirit of victory over sin.

Charles Finney, in his *Revival Lectures,* wrote that "a revival breaks the power of the world and of sin over Christians."[1] Finney is underscoring the same truth the apostle John was. "When the Lord is near," Finney writes, "the charm of the world is broken, and the power of sin overcome."

Now this is no great revelation. Even neophyte Christians know that sin quickly diminishes one's eagerness for Christ to show up. It's like the experience of Eden all over again— men and women hiding from God's presence. On the other hand, maturing Christians understand that a consistent walk in righteousness is an invitation for the Lord to draw delightfully close. Paradise is near again.

Please don't misunderstand. I'm not writing about perfection, and neither is the apostle John. In his discussion about knowing fellowship with Christ, he includes these words upfront: "If we confess our sins, he is faithful and just, and will forgive our sins and cleanse us from all unrighteousness" (1 John 1:9). This indicates John's realization of man and woman's need for ongoing spiritual renewal.

My experience is that such a prayer of confession needs to be practiced quite regularly; our own humanity is simply too potent for us to go without it for long. Even the strongest of believers falls short of what he or she wants to be. Fatigue causes us to drop our spiritual guard. Circumstances overwhelm us, or we're blindsided by the enemy. Our proclivity to failure should make us thank the Lord for the opportunity for daily times of confession and the cleansing it brings.

Unfortunately, far more Christians can define confession than actually practice it. Why?

My guess is they're not that conscious of their need to consistently walk in the light. Like the society of which they're a part, they excuse their sins. They reason that 70 or 80 percent light-walking should be adequate; the remaining 20 to 30 percent darkness-stepping should be overlooked by the Lord.

They unconsciously revise John's description about God's being light and in Him there being no darkness at all. They rationalize that they can still have fellowship with Him as long as they don't drop much below the previously suggested percentages. Sensing no need to confess their sins each day, they lose the opportunity of regularly realigning themselves with God's 100 percent standard. Confession is for really negligent Christians, they figure; those 30 or 40 percent light-walkers with a 60 or 70 percent darkness factor.

Sadly, because of sin, most people functionally prostitute away that wonderful sense of their Lord's closeness that's so nurturing and so satisfying to those who regularly taste it.

Confession is a profound simplicity. One must first keep in mind that, after we sin, Calvary is the place to meet Christ again. I go there through prayer. I find it helps to kneel, picturing myself at the base of the cross, taking the time necessary in my head to put aside my immediate surroundings and to concentrate on that pivotal scene around which all of history turns.

Before praying anything, I purposely bring to mind the broken body of my Lord hanging on that ugly gibbet. Then I bow my head and prepare to speak. My prayers of confession often go something like this:

"Jesus, I'm back here again.

"It wasn't intentional. I just got to talking and laughing, and I didn't guard what I said. My words about Pete weren't constructive—or, for that matter, even fair.

"I don't know why I always seem to go after him. Give me insight into this. I do know I've asked You to forgive me for this specific sin too many times now. I'm thankful, anyway, that it's been awhile since I've erred like this.

"Jesus, please don't allow what I said to harm Pete or to get back to him and discourage him. I believe You're also going to have to give me Your supernatural love for him, because humanly I don't really like him that much.

"It's Your blood, Christ, that cleanses me from all sin. Cover this one also, will You please? I'm sorry, truly sorry for how sin mars me and others, and most of all, for how it hurts you.

"It's not my intent ever to do this again.

"Thank You for forgiving me and for cleansing me from this unrighteousness. I want to learn to see others, including Pete, the way You see them, and always to walk in the same way You walked. Amen."

If you have little experience with confession, it stands to reason that you're also not experiencing the close fellowship with Christ about which John writes. And woe to the church that's filled with people who live confessionless lives— a congregation like this loses all touch with God's standard of holiness.

Remember, when a majority of Christians in a given church have become comfortable walking in the half-light, it is a clear indication that revival is needed. We may lower the standards, but God does not. Though we settle for a low median, God refuses to establish a righteousness norm by the curve. Listen! Jesus may again be knocking outside the church door.

The older I get and the better acquainted I am with Christ, the more I'm aware of His insistence on holiness. This seems to be a matter about which He's not open to negotiation even in the slightest.

I guess somebody could consider bringing up this subject for discussion, "Ah, Jesus, I feel You're a bit too stubborn on this righteousness issue. I mean, I figure I've made some pretty big concessions Your way. On the matter of this one pet sin, couldn't You compromise a little? Accommodate me? Maybe 3 or 4 percent darkness allowable, and all the rest light?"

I warn you, the Lord won't budge even one millimeter. The privilege of drawing close to Christ in fellowship carries with it this conviction that Jesus feels strongly about the necessity for holiness. Revival and righteousness are inextricably linked.

Recently I counseled with someone who's struggling with a difficult temptation faced by many. This man was contrite in spirit; he really wanted help with his problem. Knowing that his inadequate background would make overcoming his temptation a battle royal, I almost said, "Understanding all you've told me, I'm not sure I can predict that you'll make it." (How glad I am that I didn't say what I felt!)

In church that very next Sunday, during the communion, our pastor repeated the words of a leading fourth-century churchman, the great Bishop Basil.

"Christ lived as one of us . . ." said our pastor in his prayer of thanks for the bread and the wine, quoting the ancient Basil. Then came this marvelous phrase: "Christ lived as one of us, *yet without sin.*" The words struck me with great force—"yet without sin."

On the way home, I shared with my family how God at that moment had spoken to me in a special way. Jesus didn't sin, not even once. The thought overwhelmed me when I thought about the man with whom I had counseled. And none of us, no matter our backgrounds, need sin either. Yes, this person was weak. But now, by the Holy Spirit, this same sinless Christ indwelt my friend—indwells us all.

"In him [Christ] there is no sin," writes the apostle John. But he didn't stop there, he went on: "No one who abides in him sins" (1 John 3:5–6). So whatever the temptation or temptations that plague us —and all of us are weak in one way or another, and all of us are frustrated that we seem so incapable of knowing consistent victory—we do well to remember that in Christ we have every option to overcome. We are not helpless victims, endlessly victimized. We *can* know victory, *and in a far shorter period of time than most people suspect.*

The absolute truth is: Anyone who wants to be close friends with Christ needs to achieve this victory-over-sin mindset, needs to learn to keep short accounts with God, needs to refuse to allow sins of long standing to go unconfessed day after day, week after week, even year after year.

"Wait, David," you say, "here we were discussing fellowship with Christ—you know, eating together at church potlucks; the two of us being close friends, chummy; the whole congregation knowing divine closeness—and all of a sudden you bring up my areas of weakness, temptations, failures, the things that really embarrass me. What gives?"

I believe that humans can have a holy friendship in our churches with the divine Christ, but the friendship or fellowship will never be on our terms—"old buddies"—with us defining the relationship we want with God.

In C. S. Lewis's *Chronicles of Narnia,* the Christ figure is Aslan the lion. He can be gentle and play and romp, "But be careful," warns the writer, "he's not a tame lion, you know!" With this warning, Lewis helps his readers understand that this gentle personality has an awesome side that needs to be respected, even feared.

The truth Lewis captures figuratively is consistent with the picture of Christ we find in the Scriptures. Yes, Jesus is a friend who sticks closer than a brother, and we can know intimacy with Him, but He's also Lion of the Tribe of Judah, the Holy One of God, Deliverer from Sin. And consequently, He commands our reverence.

Unfortunately, some of those closest to the Lord had to learn this lesson the hard way. Who worshiped like King David, a man after God's own heart? But David, through dramatic failure, discovered that this privilege of being God's intimate was not to be taken for granted.

Who knew fellowship with God like Adam? But even walking with his Creator in the garden didn't insulate him from being judged for his disobedience.

Who's been a member of a church that could possibly compare to the one in Acts 5? Yet being part of such a congregation and living so close to the powerful actuality of the risen Christ resulted in destruction rather than safety for Ananias and Sapphira when they lived a lie.

Obviously, walking with God doesn't grant allowance for laxity regarding sin, even though such an unconscious attitude seems to characterize many in the church today.

When Israel ceased being a positive influence on the surrounding nations and began instead to be influenced by the sins of these pagan cultures, the people of God started to stare annihilation in the face. In similar desperate fashion, when the church of our day manifests the same sins as the ungodly society of which she is a part, she invites God's judgment.

When her marriages no longer hold; when her people are marked by greed and the love of money; when God's sabbath principle is consistently violated; when the fear of other people becomes greater than the fear of God; when conversations center on entertainment and restaurants and sports and seldom if ever on the advancement of the kingdom; when believers' consciences are no longer tender; when quarrels and divisions and jealousies abound; when good causes lack Christian support or fail for lack of Christian involvement; when only a handful are interested in the conversion of souls here at home, and mission reports are considered boring— when this is the contemporary church profile, don't boast about the latest building plans, don't brag about charitable giving and beneficial tax writeoffs, don't bother with denominational growth reports through mergers. Ask instead why the presence of the Lord isn't being sensed more—and whether current problems are like those of ancient Israel.

Yes, we, the present people of God, want the Lord. But too often we want our pet sins even more:

- Pampering that driving inner need to be recognized as someone important.
- Selfishly protecting what we've worked hard to achieve, to buy, to gain; viewing these commodities as our own and considering kingdom imperatives as optional.
- Nurturing private sexual fantasies.
- Becoming incrementally accustomed to deceit.
- Manipulating to get our way, regardless of whomever is violated in the process.
- Excusing laziness and self-indulgence.
- Ignoring our present national moral decay and negligently assuming that somehow, in some way, even without a holy church, all will miraculously turn out okay.
- Loving this present life. ("Do not love the world or the things in the world. If any one loves the world, love for the Father is not in him," 1 John 2:15.)

The hour must come when the church as a body and the individuals who compose the corporate entity reach for holiness. We must ask God for determination to overcome sin; we must pray for conviction for our unrighteousness. We must understand that we will never experience that overwhelming sense of the presence of Christ if we are not intent on striving to be 100 percent light-walkers. And particularly in these days, we need to pray:

"Lord, have mercy."

"Lord, have mercy on the church."

"Lord, have mercy on me."

For Discussion and Reflection

1. "Woe to me! . . . For I am a man of unclean lips, and I live among a people of unclean lips, and my eyes have seen the King, the Lord Almighty." This was the prophet's response in Isaiah 6 after seeing the Lord (v. 5, NIV). If you became keenly aware of the Lord's presence, how do you think you would describe your own life and our contemporary day?

2. What temptation have you learned to overcome in the past year?

3. Tears often characterize times of revival in the church. Why is this?

4. Time is seldom allotted for private or corporate confession of sin in our church services. Why is this?

5. Psalm 24:3 asks: "Who may ascend the hill of the Lord? Who may stand in his holy place?" (NIV). Do you know the psalmist's answer? Turn to the Scripture and attempt to paraphrase the response in modern terms.

Readings

IN ALL OLD TESTAMENT REVIVALS there was a deep sense of sin and an overpowering desire to separate themselves from it and from all its sponsoring causes. Such divinely induced anxiety and agonizing conviction of sin needs no prompting or psychological maneuvering. The work is uniquely that of the Holy Spirit. The failures of the past, even those that have been forgotten, suddenly become so real and so painfully present that no amount of comfort or personal rationalization will assuage the terrible pressure of individual guilt and heartbreak. Accordingly, so spontaneous and thorough should be the conviction and simultaneous hatred of sin that there will be no need to plead with men and women to make any decisions.

—Walter C. Kaiser, Jr., *Quest for Renewal: Personal Revival in the Old Testament*, pp. 20–21

MENEHELISI [in the Solomon Islands, 1970] was the most unlikely place for revival. Unlike Malu'u, there was no real spiritual hunger; many of the people were hardened nominal Christians, some hiding serious sins, many were cold towards God, full of divisive bitterness. The pastor himself was very far from God, two-faced, and a constant hindrance behind the scenes.

After the meetings on the first Sunday, it was apparent that the Holy Spirit was moving among the people. A tremendous release came upon them. In the large leaf-thatched church, almost the whole company of 150 men, women and children rose to their feet and began praying, oblivious of each other. This had never happened in the Solomons before. As they did so, conviction of sin came upon them. This continued every evening for several weeks. Sometimes publicly and sometimes in private, confessions began to pour out in an endless stream. The Spirit of God continued to work in their hearts until they found relief before God in confession— often of things hidden for years. One woman confessed to serious sins committed in Queensland which had hindered her Christian experience for over 30 years.

Even the spiritual pastors, men of God from villages nearby who thought they knew the situation, were shocked. Things had been far worse than anyone had imagined. For instance, in Menehelisi, a Christian village, numerous cases of adultery were brought to light.

Heber Houenimae, who was visiting Menehelisi for that time, wrote years afterwards of his clear memories: "When the missionary gave the message, it really cut like a knife. It really broke down the heart. People were convicted of sin and came looking for Jesus. . . ."

—Alison Griffiths, *Fire in the Islands!:*
The Acts of the Holy Spirit in the Solomons, pp. 111–112

REPENTANCE is a thorough housecleaning. As far as we are concerned, there is a complete turning from sin. Not only must confession be made to God, but we must be willing to do all we can to make things right with people we have wronged. If we try to trim the corners, and excuse a few favorite shortcomings, we are fooling ourselves. No revival can come in our hearts until sin is out of the way. Furthermore, until this is true of our lives, we stand in the way of God's blessing to others.

The great revival that came to the New Hebrides Islands in 1949 is a splendid example. Led by their minister, a little group of earnest Christians entered into a covenant with God that they would "give Him no rest until He had made

Jerusalem a praise in the earth." Months passed, but nothing happened. Then one night a young man arose from his knees and read from Psalm 24: "Who shall ascend unto the hill of the Lord? or who shall stand in his holy place? He that hath clean hands and a pure heart. . . . He shall receive the blessing from the Lord . . ." (vs. 3–5). The young man closed his Bible, and looking at his companions on their knees, said: "Brethren, it is just so much humbug to be waiting thus night after night, month after month, if we ourselves are not right with God. I must ask myself, 'Is my heart pure? Are my hands clean?'"[2]

As the men faced this question, they fell on their faces in confession and consecration. That night revival came to the town. The whole community was shaken by the power of God, and within a few weeks the revival had moved across the island sweeping literally thousands of people into the Kingdom.

—Robert E. Coleman, *Dry Bones Can Live Again:
Revival in the Local Church*, pp. 34–35

— ◆ —

TO SUCH A PLACE came the Rev. James McGready, who had been well converted during the sporadic revivals of the 1780s and who had been impressed by the movement that originated in Hampden-Sydney College in 1787. McGready had been ordained a Presbyterian minister, but served as a pastoral evangelist in North Carolina. James McGready's appearance was unprepossessing, his voice tremulous and coarse, his gestures uncouth, and his manner inelegant. It was said that he was so ugly that he attracted attention on the street. But he possessed such a zeal and earnestness that his handicaps were soon forgotten in his preaching.

In North Carolina, McGready's ministry had provoked reviving or resentment. In 1796, McGready accepted the pastorate of three small Kentucky churches.[3] As he was intensely

committed to the Concert of Prayer, he signed up many intercessors for a covenant devoting half an hour at sunset Satur-
days and half an hour at sunrise Sundays to intreaty for an
outpouring of the Spirit. This local concert of prayer continued for three years, until its intercessors were overtaken by
night and day counsel of sinners.

At Red River, in July of 1798, the Lord's Supper was cele-
brated, and the accumulation of prayer together with the
powerful preaching produced a great solemnity.[4] The boldest
and most daring sinners were reduced to tearful conviction.
On the last Sunday in August, McGready was assisting John
Rankin at Gasper River, and many hearers were prostrated,
groaning in their conviction. This spirit of conviction ebbed
and flowed for a couple of years, at the same time that the
widespread awakening in New England was raising up intercessors for the west.[5]

"The winter of 1799," said McGready, "was for the most
part a time of weeping and mourning with the children of
God." During the summer of 1800, all previous revivals in
the area seemed nothing more than a few scattering drops
before a mighty rain."[6] The great awakening in the west had
begun, changing the frontier and the nation.

—J. Edwin Orr, *The Eager Feet:*
Evangelical Awakenings, 1790–1830, p. 60

HOW CAN THE intense conviction of sin which occurs in all
evangelical awakenings be explained? For conviction of sin
there is, and it seems to smite almost everyone within the
sound of the human voice or within the sphere of influence.
Indeed, it may be felt beyond the sound of the voice and
away from physical lines of communication. At the very moment that the spirit of confession was poured out upon
Wheaton's chapel assembly [1950], a Wheaton College Glee
Club was touring in Florida, when a student called out "Stop

the bus!"[7] When the bus pulled over at the side of the road, he unburdened himself of a breach of trust, and a chain reaction began in the membership of the choir so far from home. This kind of thing has occurred again and again in revival history.

—J. Edwin Orr, *Campus Aflame: Dynamic of Student Religious Revolution; Evangelical Awakenings in Collegiate Communities*, p. 219

— ◆ —

CLEANSE ME

SEARCH ME, O GOD, and know my heart today;
Try me, O Savior, know my thoughts, I pray:
See if there be some wicked way in me:
Cleanse me from every sin and set me free.
I praise Thee, Lord, for cleansing me from sin:
Fulfill Thy Word, and make me pure within;
Fill me with fire, where once I burned with shame:
Grant my desire to magnify Thy name. . . .
O Holy Ghost, revival comes from Thee:
Send a revival—start the work in me:
Thy Word declares Thou wilt supply our need:
For blessing now, O Lord, I humbly plead.

— Edwin Orr, in *Inspiring Hymns*, p. 60

5

To Serve the King

— ◆ —

I KEEP A HYMNAL in my desk at the office. For many years I've made it a point sometime around the noon hour to read two hymns, and in the course of a year I usually work my way through a good-sized hymnal. I've gone through Presbyterian, Baptist, Anglican, and Independent renditions, traditional formats and contemporary styles.

Now, this is not just a surface reading. My custom is to consider the words slowly and thoughtfully. Quite frequently I take notes on some of the hymn texts; this way I have files available regarding songs that fit various subjects about which I might some day preach.

In the course of many years, I've come to notice the many different ways the hymn writers picture Christ. Sometimes He's a shepherd. In other songs He's the lamb, such as "The Lamb Is the Light of the City of God." A hymn which picks up on the second picture in the previous title is "The Light of the World Is Jesus."

Most often—and I'm quite confident this is accurate because I've been doing this for some years—the picture of Christ referred to in these hymns is that of a king: "King of my life I crown Thee now . . ." or "Lives again our glorious King, alleluia . . ." or "At the name of Jesus every knee shall bow; every tongue confess Him King of glory now."

Then of course there are other themes related to Christ's kingship—such as "Crown Him with many crowns, the Lamb upon His throne"; "Jesus shall reign . . ."; "Thou didst leave Thy throne and Thy kingly crown"; and on and on.

The theme of the Lord as King is also strongly emphasized in the Bible, particularly in the Old Testament. From Psalm 47:7–8: "For God is King of all the earth; sing praises with a psalm! God reigns over the nations; God sits on his holy throne." From Psalm 24:7 (also in v. 9) "Lift up your heads,

89

O gates! and be lifted up, O ancient doors! That the King of glory may come in."

In the Gospels, we see Christ refusing to allow the people to make Him king on their own terms, but there's no question that He saw himself as King. Without a doubt, His basic message was the announcement of His Kingdom—or, said differently, His kingship!

An Old Testament prophet had predicted, "Your King comes to you . . . humble and mounted upon an ass" (Zech. 9:9). At birth, wise men from the east came asking, "Where is he who has been born king of the Jews?" (Matt. 2:2). And at death, as He hung on the cross, a sign above His head proclaimed, "This is Jesus the King of the Jews" (Matt. 27:37). A passage in Revelation about His future return to earth reveals His name to be "King of kings and Lord of lords" (19:16)!

Certainly Christ's closest followers picked up on this truth that He was a king. Peter's words are, "We were eyewitnesses of his majesty!" (2 Pet. 1:16). John declared Christ to be "the ruler of kings on earth" (Rev. 1:5). And Paul wrote (echoed in the hymn I mentioned previously), "at the name of Jesus Christ every knee should bow, in heaven and on earth and under the earth" (Phil. 2:10).

Quite naturally, it follows that the King and His kingdom were an important part of the message that the early church proclaimed. Following the preaching of Paul and Silas in Thessalonica, the rabble cried out, "These men . . . are . . . acting against the decrees of Caesar, saying there is another king, Jesus!" (Acts 17:6–7). Well, the rabble got it right! Or at least they had listened and accurately heard what had been declared to them.

Returning to the premise of this book: Are you one who's having trouble experiencing Christ's presence in His church on Sundays? As a starting point, why not attempt to picture Him as your King? I am not suggesting that you fabricate a fiction. Whether or not you choose to reflect on it, the truth is that Jesus is not only your King, but King of the entire universe!

What I'm suggesting is that when you sing,

> Jesus shall reign where'er the sun
> Does his successive journeys run;
> His kingdom spread from shore to shore,
> Till moons shall wax and wane no more,[1]

you intentionally picture in your mind what it is you're singing. To fail to imagine the reality of your musical witness —that Jesus shall reign—is to be involved in meaningless ritual. You might as well sing, "la la-la-la, la-la-la, la-la-la."

I believe we do well, when entering the church sanctuary for a service, to prepare for worship by making ourselves conscious of being in the presence of our great King. Unlike in the days of the psalmist, when pageantry was part of worship ritual, today believers tend to enter the Lord's courts with too little respect for our Sovereign. They would give much more forethought to entering the oval office of the President, or the office of a prime minister or of a governor— or in some cases even to meeting with the chief executive officer of their place of employment.

Is Jesus really with us on Sundays?

Is He truly a great king?

I know Christ is a friend, and a brother, and our Savior. But is He also our King? And are we His subjects? Or is it just the wind that's subject to His commands? Demons maybe? Angels, yes! But not people?

"Religious symbolism," someone scoffs. "Kings and thrones and crowns. That symbol might have aided past generations in their worship, but it went out of style when the power of earthly kings began to wane. It's anachronistic, so why not drop it?"

Is that how you think? Perhaps a better question would be: Is that how you act? Is the truth about Christ as our reigning Monarch so removed from where you live or make a living that Christ's kingship really has no immediate relevancy?

I ask these questions because I have been encouraging us to see Christ as present in His church. And picturing Him as

King prepares us to understand another of the ways His presence can be measured. I believe that loyal subjects, *when truly conscious of their King's presence,* think more in terms of service than of being served.

A *true* servant of a good king doesn't spend priority time thinking about whether the ruler is making him as comfortable and as fulfilled as he wants. His first question isn't, "During this Sunday visit with my lord, will all my needs be met?" "Is it going to be worth my while to have invested a portion of my time with my monarch?" "Will my being here put me in the king's good graces?"

If we can distance ourselves from the routine of church attendance to examine our motives for this Sunday habit, we may discover self-centeredness to be the attitude of a large number of Christ's subjects! In fact, I'm convinced this disposition accurately describes a majority of people who attend church week after week. How they can serve their King is the farthest thing from their minds.

In 1960, a whole nation responded positively to President-inaugurate John F. Kennedy when he said, "Ask not what your country can do for you; ask what you can do for your country." Few, if any, replied, "Just who does he think he is—ah, forget it, pal!" No, at the time, Kennedy's personal popularity added to the respect Americans had for the office he held and made his request seem not only reasonable but right.

But woe to the current reign of the monarch Jesus if His subjects' attitude is one of "Ask not what we can do for the kingdom, but ask what the kingdom can do for us." How successful can the church be if this is the prevailing mindset? And what folly it is for church leaders to accommodate such thinking, killing themselves trying to satisfy a people who already have far more than their fair share of what the world has to offer?

Conversely, when there is an overwhelming sense of the Lord's presence in the church, when Christ is perceived to be who He really is, when a time of genuine revival is known, there is always a great burst of holy enthusiasm as it relates to service. During revival, people consider it a privilege to be involved in their King's service.

It's tough for a boss to build a successful business with employees whose only thoughts are of, "How are we workers going to benefit?" A successful marriage is hard to create when both partners keep asking selfishly, "Why isn't my mate better at meeting my needs?" A coach won't succeed if the players are only interested in their own personal advancement, in their careers' being spotlighted and their private salaries' increased, rather than in how to make sacrifices for the good of the team.

Likewise, a pastor will not experience a truly successful church if the basic mindset of his members remains, "What's in this for me?"

Oh, he might get them to sing heartily on a Sunday morning,

> Rise up, O men of God!
> Have done with lesser things;
> Give heart and soul and mind and strength
> To serve the King of kings.[2]

But singing and doing can be quite different matters. And was there ever a day in North America when believers needed more to be done with lesser things?

For example, what church can rise higher than its prayer base? Prayer is vital for spiritual advancement. Christians all know this in their heads. Even so, lesser priorities continue to take precedence over private and corporate times of intercession.

Again, when has the church ever moved forward without sacrifice? When have programs of social mercy been launched, new mission fields opened for the gospel, or times of genuine revival been experienced without self-denial on the part of God's people? Sadly, relatively few in the church today have much stomach for putting aside personal desires.

A plague of sexual perversity has swept this continent. We

sowed to the wind, and now we're reaping the whirlwind. Even our milk cartons carry the pictures of missing children. We eat cereal in the morning and look at their faces—who knows the horror of their fates? Yet many church people find it too inconvenient to boycott stores that make huge profits on the sale of published pornographic filth which researchers directly link to child sexual abuse.

Most Christians have some working familiarity with the statistics on abortion in this land. But those involved in the prolife movement will testify that one of the biggest battles they face is the apathy of local congregations.

But we're singing so well!—verse 3 now:

> Rise up, O men of God!
> The church for you doth wait,
> Her strength unequal to her task;
> Rise up, and make her great![3]

As we sing, I believe we do well to remind ourselves how Christ never gave people the satisfaction of declaring Him King on their own terms.

"Jesus, we affirm Your kingship. Show us the multiplying-fish-and-loaves trick again!"

"Jesus, I'll throw my weight behind Your cause if You'll only retract what You said about selling all I have and giving it to the poor."

"Jesus, You're King, and we're among the three closest of Your subjects. Let us have the positions of eternal prominence. Let us sit at Your left and at Your right so everyone will notice and admire us."

Christ's answer was a firm negative to all such demands.

Don't misunderstand. Jesus was a king, all right, and for those who bowed their knee to Him there would be decided benefits. In fact, at the very genesis of His ministry, Christ announced, "I bring you good news! In what kingdom before have the poor or the poor in spirit ever been blest? Never has this been the case with the worldly kings you've known. But in the kingdom I'm announcing, the poor are truly blessed because they are of personal concern to the king!

"Who listening to Me is part of a kingdom where comfort is offered to those who mourn?

"What earthly monarch rewards those who labor and toil for goodness, for righteousness? What despot rewards those who give mercy?

"Listen to Me carefully: in My kingdom those who mourn, those who hunger for justice, those who show mercy—all these will be blessed.

"And for those who are pure, not just in outward actions but in their very most inward selves, I tell you truly, they will see God. What greater blessing can anyone want? And I promise to provide this for those who enter into My Kingdom" (my paraphrase of Matt. 5:3–8).

Great promises, aren't they?—and these are just a sample of the revolutionary benefits we too often take for granted. Subjects of Christ aren't victims of a rapacious dictator. Here's a King for the people of the world, for the poor of the earth, for the peace seekers—One who is enormously equipped to rule in a way that is beyond the capabilities of any monarch who has ever reigned.

However, we must realize that there are expectations on Christ's part for our enjoyment of these benefits. He gave us very specific commands about how we are to serve Him. We each need to bow our knee before this King and say, "I acknowledge You, Christ, as rightful Lord. I have been a rebellious subject. But now I admit that Your way is the right way, and my way has been the wrong way. Though I don't deserve it, I thank You for offering to accept me into Your kingdom, And yes, I am willing to obey Your commands."

Two key commands of Christ's, especially, enter on how He expects us to serve Him. They can be found in Mark 12:30: "The first is, 'You shall love the Lord your God with all your heart, and with all your soul, and with all your mind, and with all your strength.' The second is this, 'You shall love your neighbor as yourself.'"

So serving our king means that we are to show "king's love" for God and for others, just as He shows it to us. More often than not, loving is the exact opposite of asking, "What's in this for me?" Loving means looking out for the good of others the way most look out for their own good. Loving means serving the King by serving His subjects.

That's the lifestyle the King had in mind for His followers. It's a concept so utterly simple that it is utterly profound. If everyone in the world lived this way, our major societal problems would all be solved overnight. Imagine the revolutionary potential in the world if only those who call themselves Christian would live this way! How wonderful it would be if serving others, especially those in need, was considered normal for life in the kingdom! Once the mindset among those who bow to Christ is one of serving, not of being served—of what can I give, not what do I get—it is a whole new day for the cause.

Self-centeredness must not be the bottom line with the subjects of this divine King. Even if the rest of the world exercises me-first practices, in Christ's church it has to be different. Jesus asks in Luke 17,

> Will any one of you, who has a servant plowing or keeping sheep, say to him when he has come in from the field, "Come at once and sit down at table"? Will he not rather say to him, "Prepare supper for me, and gird yourself and *serve* me, till I eat and drink; and afterward you shall eat and drink"? . . . So you also, when you have done all that is commanded you, say, "We are unworthy servants; we have only done what was our duty" (vv. 7–10).

These strong words need to be placed paramount in the minds of those who serve the King. If He were physically present in church on Sunday, if we could actually see Him, then whoever rendered service or contributed to the cause would not insist on reward, recognition, or favor, but would declare, "Your Majesty, I have only done what was my duty!"

What we need then is for Christ to be more present in his church. That divine presence would put a stop to all the cajoling and pampering and making over people to motivate them to serve. The truth is that loyal subjects, when conscious of being in their King's presence, think in terms of service more than of being served. And so service on the King's behalf is another measurement that the church is successfully doing what it was intended to do.

That's why I continue to preach revival. For during times of genuine revival in the church, the overwhelming sense of the presence of the Lord quickly vanquishes all tendencies to self-serving Christian discipleship.

"David, your such a johnny-one-note!" people have sometimes said. "Why be negative about the church? Jettison the revival theme. Concentrate on the positive."

But I *am* concentrating on the good—and the better, and the best. That is what I intend to keep on doing. The church can know no greater good than an extended visit from the King before whom she bows.

But is this One not already among us, Sunday after Sunday, unrecognized by those who gather for worship? One of those noontime hymns I frequently read, one written by Charles Spurgeon, perfectly expresses this fact:

> Amidst us our beloved stands,
> And bids us view his pierced hands,
> Points to the wounded feet and side,
> Blest emblems of the crucified.
>
> If now with eyes defiled and dim,
> We see the signs but see not Him
> O may his love the scales displace,
> And bid us see Him face to face
>
> Thou glorious bridegroom of our hearts
> Thy present smile a heaven imparts.
> O, lift the veil, if veil there be,
> Let every saint thy glory see.
>
> AMEN

And how can we help but serve such a King!

For Discussion and Reflection

1. Which of the following questions is more dominant in the thinking of North American Christians:

   > Is Christ serving me well?
   > Am I serving Christ well?

2. Pretend King Jesus posted a list of all in your church who served Him well during the last month. Would your name be included? Why or why not?

3. Would having Christ bodily present in your congregation make it easier or harder to get people to volunteer for Sunday ministry positions such as singing in the choir, ushering, nursery service, teaching Sunday School, etc.?

4. Name at least five ways to serve the Lord in your daily work setting.

5. Why should the poor and the powerless always benefit when revival sweeps through the church?

Readings

REVIVALISM is generally understood in terms of the dramatic conversion of profligate sinners, but such an image is not true to the literal meaning of "revival." [Charles G.] Finney's message was directed primarily to church people or "professors of religion" not living up to the fullness of Christian existence. . . . But this call to a "revived" Christian life incorporated the implicit demand that true conversion evidence itself in good works and commitment to the welfare of others. In such dynamics is the beginning of an impulse to reform activity. . . .

For Finney the essence of sin was selfishness. Such concern for one's own welfare was directly contradicted by God's character, especially the attribute of benevolence. To be "converted" for Finney was to forsake one's own interests for the sake of others. This reflection of God's benevolence in the life of the convert would evidence itself in "doing good" to all and becoming as "useful" as possible in the world. The natural outlet in Finney's time for such impulses was a series of "benevolent societies" set up for every conceivable philanthropy and social crusade. Finney's converts threw themselves into such work. . . .

In his *Lectures on Revivals of Religion* Finney argued that "revivals are hindered when ministers and *churches take wrong ground in regard to any question involving human rights.*" He applied this particularly to slavery, insisting that "the church cannot turn away from this question." . . .

In Finney's own words, "One of the reasons for the low state of religion at the present time, is that many churches have taken the wrong side on the subject of slavery, have suffered prejudice to prevail over principle, and have feared to call this abomination by its true name." . . . Though Finney refused to disrupt the church practices of others, he affirmed that "where I *have authority*, I exclude slaveholders from the [Lord's Supper], and I will as long as I live."

—Donald W. Dayton, *Discovering an Evangelical Heritage*, pp. 18–19

— ◆ —

THE SHARP CLEAVAGE between the clergy and the laity has made it convenient for the laity to squirm out of the responsibilities of teaching, exhortation, witnessing, et cetera. They sometimes reason like this: We aren't trained, and the pastor is (or rather, is supposed to be); we don't have time, and of course, the pastor does (he is paid to do the work of the ministry); we don't have spiritual gifts, whereas the pastor has them all. . . .

The revival [in western Canada, 1971] knocked a hole through such warped views. The clergy and the laity both saw themselves for what they were: sinners, accepted by Jesus Christ and empowered by the Holy Spirit to do the work of God on earth. The awakening in Saskatoon and other cities was a revival of the layman. . . .

Laymen all over the revival area woke up to the biblical truth that they were God's ambassadors. Their pastor was, after all, made of the same clay as they, and if God could use him, God could use them too. In some instances whole congregations were moved from dead center to catch a glimpse of their contribution to the Body of Christ.

Of course, many Christians were actively serving God before the revival came. There has always been the company of the committed who have seen themselves as full time Christians—God's representatives in every situation in life. But the revival caused their number to increase. . . .

Burning with the zeal of those who had a fresh touch from the living God, laymen began to witness. Their testimonies ignited sparks in one church after another. To the surprise of many, the laymen often became more effective than the pastor in bringing revival to other churches.

One pastor who visited the Saskatoon revival returned to his church to tell what God had done in his life. The congregation was unmoved. The next weekend lay people spoke at the same church and half the congregation came forward, including the pastor.

—Erwin W. Lutzer, *Flames of Freedom*, pp. 66–67

— ◆ —

[AN EXCITING illustration concerning the importance of lay involvement in ministry is found in this account of how the famous minister D. L. Moody came to know the Lord:]

In the midst of the revival, on Saturday morning, April 21st, 1855, Edward Kimball walked out of his lodgings at America House, having "decided to speak to Moody about Christ and about his soul. I started down town to Holton's shoe store. When I was nearly there I began to wonder whether I ought to go just then during business hours. And I thought maybe my mission might embarrass the boy, that when I went away the other clerks might ask who I was, and when they learned might taunt Moody and ask if I was trying to make a good boy out of him. While I was pondering over it all I passed the store without noticing it. Then, when I found I had gone by the door I determined to make a dash for it and have it over at once."

He found Moody in the back part wrapping up shoes in paper and stacking them on shelves. "I went up to him and put my hand on his shoulder, and as I leaned over I placed my foot upon a shoe box." Looking down into Moody's eyes he made what he thought afterwards a very weak plea. Neither could ever recall the exact words but "I asked him to come to Christ, who loved him and who wanted his love and should have it." There were tears in Kimball's eyes.

"It seemed," Kimball records, "that the young man was just ready for the light that broke upon him, for there, at once, in the back of that shoe store in Boston," Moody "gave himself and his life to Christ."

Kimball slipped from the store a few minutes after he had entered.

Next morning, Sunday, as Moody came out of his room over the shut-up shop, "I thought the old sun shone a good deal brighter than it ever had before—I thought that it was just smiling upon me; and as I walked out upon Boston Common and heard the birds singing in the trees, I thought they were all singing a song to me. Do you know, I fell in love with the birds. I had never cared for them before. It seemed to me that I was in love with all creation. I had not a bitter feeling against any man, and I was ready to take all men to my heart."

—J. C. Pollock, *Moody: A Biographical Portrait of the Pacesetter in Modern Mass Evangelism*, pp. 13–14

— ◆ —

[SERVICE RENDERED Christ should not be thought of as being only that which happens at church. Here from a famous novel is an example of Christ's presence touching the workplace as well:]

Norman looked at Clark thoughtfully. The managing editor was a member of a church of a different denomination from that of Norman's. The two men had never talked together on religious matters although they had been associated on the paper for several years.

"Come in here a minute, Clark, and shut the door," said Norman.

Clark came in and the two men faced each other alone. Norman did not speak for a minute. Then he said abruptly:

"Clark, if Christ was editor of a daily paper, do you honestly think He would print three columns and a half of prize fight in it?"

"No, I don't suppose He would."

"Well, that's my only reason for shutting this account out of the *News*. I have decided not to do a thing in connection with the paper for a whole year that I honestly believe Jesus would not do."

Clark could not have looked more amazed if the chief had suddenly gone crazy. In fact, he did think something was wrong, though. Mr. Norman was one of the last men in the world, in his judgment, to lose his mind.

"What effect will that have on the paper?" he finally managed to ask in a faint voice.

"What do you think?" asked Norman with a keen glance.

"I think it will simply ruin this paper," replied Clark promptly. He was gathering up his bewildered senses, and began to remonstrate, "Why, it isn't feasible to run a paper nowadays on any such basis. It's too ideal. The world isn't ready for it. You can't make it pay. Just as sure as you live, if you shut out this prize fight report you will lose hundreds of subscribers. It doesn't take a prophet to see that. The very best people in town are eager to read it. They know it has taken place, and when they get the paper this evening they will expect half a page at least. Surely, you can't afford to disregard the wishes of the public to such an extent. It will be a great mistake if you do, in my opinion."

Norman sat silent a minute. Then he spoke gently but firmly.

"Clark, what in your honest opinion is the right standard for determining conduct? Is the only right standard for every one, the probable action of Jesus Christ? Would you say that the highest, best law for a man to live by was contained in asking the question, 'What would Jesus do?' And then doing it regardless of results? In other words, do you think men everywhere ought to follow Jesus' example as closely as they can in their daily lives?" Clark turned red, and moved uneasily in his chair before he answered the editor's question.

"Why—yes—I suppose if you put it on the ground of what men ought to do there is no other standard of conduct. But the question is, What is feasible? Is it possible to make it pay? To succeed in the newspaper business we have got to conform to custom and the recognized methods of society. We can't do as we would in an ideal world."

"Do you mean that we can't run the paper strictly on "Christian principles and make it succeed?"

"Yes, that's just what I mean. It can't be done. We'll go bankrupt in thirty days."

Norman did not reply at once. He was very thoughtful.

"We shall have occasion to talk this over again, Clark. Meanwhile I think we ought to understand each other frankly. I have pledged myself for a year to do everything connected with the paper after answering the question, 'What would Jesus do?' as honestly as possible. I shall continue to do this in the belief that not only can we succeed but that we can succeed better than we ever did."

—Charles M. Sheldon, *In His Steps*, pp. 26–27

EVERY PERIOD of college awakenings has been followed by a definite upsurge of missionary volunteering. In ordinary years, a number of graduates choose the foreign field, not for just a couple of years to satisfy their yen for adventure, but for life. But in times of revival, a landslide of commitments to overseas service occurs. Those not involved may shake their heads and cry "Emotionalism." Yet many of the candidates represent the most scholarly students on campus.

—J. Edwin Orr, *Campus Aflame: Dynamic of Student Religious Revolution; Evangelical Awakenings in Collegiate Communities*, p. 226

6

Preaching and Hearing the Word

— ◆ —

THE MIND IS A GIFT from God. Though it can become perverted, set in rebellion against its very Creator, leading humankind into depravity and emptiness, we nevertheless owe deep gratitude to Him for the capability of thought.

Emotions are also a gift from the Lord. How fortunate we are to be able to experience love, anger, frustration, joy, even sorrow! Often emotions can be misused as well—love can become lust, anger evolve into hatred, admiration dissolve into envy—but the fact remains that our basic emotional makeup is a remarkable gift from God.

Now, the same is true regarding the imagination. We're divinely blessed with the power to experience mentally what can't always be experienced with the senses. For example, if I ask you to imagine a cross that's as big as a church, you will instantly "see" it in your mind with next to no effort. Try it! Or you may be able to "hear" a melody you've made up in your head.

Imagination is important because it helps us understand things that are beyond what we experience with our senses. For example, when Christ talked about the kingdom of God, His hearers couldn't actually be taken to this spiritual kingdom. But the concept was still understandable to them because they were able to envision a kingdomlike situation where Christ reigned and His will was obeyed.

The truth is that it is almost impossible for most of us to think without some sort of imaginative activity. Creative people—artists, musicians, writers, craftsmen, homemakers—tend to do their work while imagining the finished product; a seamstress "sees" the finished dress, for instance, or a composer "hears" the finished song. In fact, some are unable to complete a project without imagining the finished product.

But why all this discussion about imagination? Because

throughout this book we have been imagining what would happen if Jesus were physically present in our churches.

In some quarters there is great fear of the imagination. Certain people go so far as to say it's wrong to picture God in any way, that to do so is idolatrous. This argument is as foolish as insisting that we should not use our minds because the mind can lead one into intellectual error. Such advice would be irresponsible, an advocacy of mental wastefulness—as irresponsible as insisting that God's gift of sexuality should be totally avoided because of societal perversions. We must not cast away any of these great gifts of God because of others' misuse; we need instead to use the imagination in holy ways.

Granted, human imagination has conceived of unimaginable evil. But on the other hand, worship, prayer, doing good in the world—all these begin with ideas which are accompanied in some way with imaginative activity. It is the way our minds were created and gifted to function.

As I have indicated, the use of imagination is scripturally exampled as well. The prophets frequently resorted to image-evoking words; they dramatized truth so that their hearers would take note and be lastingly affected by what they had seen and heard. The prophets told stories, painted verbal pictures, foretold the future using apocalyptic verbal imagery— appealing to the imaginations of their hearers so that truth would be translated as vividly as possible.

Nor did Jesus hesitate to have His listeners imagine God as a loving Father who, upon seeing His prodigal son return home, rushes out to greet and embrace and kiss Him.

Now, Jesus knew that God the Father is Spirit, that He does not have a body with legs and arms and lips. ("God is spirit, and his worshipers must worship in spirit and in truth," John 4:24, NIV). So why this unspiritlike picture of God? Because there's a basic resemblance between the loving actions of the father in the parable and those of our heavenly Father, and Christ wanted His hearers to see this in their minds.

I become impatient with well-meaning people who say the imagination is something to be carefully avoided when referring to God because the use of the imagination can lead to abuses.

Without a doubt, improper images of God are no less than idolatry. He is certainly not a crocodile, or a snake, or a monster—as other cultures have pictured their gods. But in spite of these improprieties, it is fallacious thinking to criticize the use of the imagination for holy purposes.

It would be like shaking a finger at the psalmist and crying "For shame, David, you won't become a man after God's own heart because you imagined your Lord as a shepherd! Such imaging of God is idolatry—the Lord is my shepherd, tut-tut."

Nonsense.

With this as background, let me share a discipline which has benefited me greatly throughout my ministry. Back when I was still pastoring, soon after walking onto the platform, I would habitually picture Christ actually coming to the Sunday service and sitting near the front where I could see Him. During the worship I would address my praise to this imagined presence, and this mental activity would underscore the awesomeness of the assignment I had been given of preaching on His behalf.

Even prior to the service, while in the process of preparing the message during the week, I pictured holding a mental conversation with the Lord about what I planned to say, to check if I had His approval. It didn't matter whether my sermon was profound or clever or captivating. What was important was that my thoughts be totally consistent with His thoughts and that my words brought Him pleasure.

I still conduct this discipline regarding my broadcasts. Often, when going over the final manuscript before recording in the studio, I deliver the message in my office "to Christ." And if changes need to be made to gain what I feel is His approval, that is fine with me. The bottom line is: Does my Lord approve of what is being said on His behalf?

You see, I don't think ministers are called by Christ just to prepare and preach human sermons. As His spokespersons, we're more than merely members of another profession.

When people attend church, there must be an encounter with the eternal Word. Times of genuine revival are always marked by God's Word coming alive again through preaching. Hearers are overwhelmed by the force of the Scriptures. Tears mark faces the way they did during the days of Nehemiah when Ezra read God's law to the people: "Then Nehemiah the governor, Ezra the priest and scribe, and the Levites who were instructing the people said to them all, 'This day is sacred to the Lord your God. Do not mourn or weep.' For all the people had been weeping as they listened to the words of the Law" (Neh. 8:9, NIV).

Preachers are to be divinely gifted and called to speak Christ's words, all the time understanding that in reality He is there, listening to what is being said. Again, that is an awesome responsibility.

After all, what is the church? Is it nothing more than manmade bricks and benches, hymnals and organs, offering reports and attendance figures, platforms for musicians and ministers to display their talents?

No, far more. The church is where the people of Jesus the Christ come to praise their Lord and to learn from Him. He is the central figure around whom all revolves. When Christ's presence is not central, the people have been cheated.

The fact that He literally is present, "in spirit and in truth, is reason enough for pastors to preach as though Christ were physically attending the church. And if He is not, then write *Ichabod* over the door.

This is what I mean. In the time of Samuel's youth, Israel was attacked by the Philistines. The two worthless and wicked sons of Eli the priest, Hophni and Phinehas, took the Ark of the Covenant into battle, thinking it would save them from their enemy. Instead, thirty thousand men of Israel were slain, and the ark was captured.

At the time, the wife of Phinehas was pregnant. First Samuel 4:19–21 reads:

When she heard the news that the ark of God had been captured and that her father-in-law and her husband were dead, she went into labor and gave birth, but was overcome by her labor pains. As she was dying, the women attending her said, "Don't despair; you have given birth to a son." But she did not respond or pay any attention. She named the boy Ichabod, saying, "The glory has departed from Israel!"—because of the capture of the ark of God and the deaths of her father-in-law and her husband (NIV).

Ichabod—the glory has departed.

I can name some incredible sanctuaries that are glorious to behold. They took years to build, but *Ichabod* is over the door. Though not carved in stone, this inscription might as well be.

Ichabod can also be written on a good number of ministers' sermon files. Oh, professionally they're preachers, and they're skilled in what they say, but they speak for themselves, not for Christ:

"How do you like my ideas, looks, humor?"

"Notice how well I match your expectations, opinions, desires!"

"Can you tell I'm important, famous, wise?"

"Will you give me your allegiance, love, and support?"

How sad when men like these are our standard for success in local ministry. To the leaders of such churches, I believe Christ pounds on the door and states, "Behold, I knock. Without My presence the glory has departed. Open the door so that I can come in."

This Sunday I want you to imagine Jesus performing a contemporary miracle. Picture Christ personally delivering the sermon at all the North American churches that profess to honor Him. Without advance publicity, with no special advertisements to attract nonattenders, the impact of His presence will nevertheless have a profound effect on these congregations.

Now what happens if Christ returns in person the following Sunday again to minister the Word miraculously from every pulpit? The congregation is more prepared for Him this time. They are eager to hear His words. Think about Him pouring out His heart about His concerns.

What do you think people will say as they leave the service and shake His hand?

"Liked your little talk a lot, Jesus!"

"Sure enjoyed what You said. It was a blessing."

I doubt this. By Christ's third or fourth consecutive visit, the weight of His words will begin to be powerfully felt. I'm not prepared to predict whether His series of messages will be positively or negatively received, but I'm convinced the overall effect will contrast decidedly with what normally occurs Sunday after Sunday.

The Scriptures show that when Christ preached, the Word of God took on great authority. Didn't our Lord's sermons have the stamp of God upon them? And didn't His sermons always demand a response of some kind from His hearers? This Lord of the universe wasn't content to dispense humdrum spiritual information or pleasant devotional thoughts— maybe to throw in an occasional "deep truth" now and then. Christ's kingdom message necessitated changes in a listener's attitude and allegiance, demanded a total commitment of resources and talents, insisted upon a willingness to devote one's life for His cause.

Wouldn't He speak like that today? And given what's happening in North America in the great battle between the kingdoms of light and darkness, I assume that Christ's present challenges would also be marked by great intensity.

Surveys show that 42 percent of the United States' population is in church or synagogue every weekend. Ministers in North America have an incredibly large pulpit. Theaters and sporting events around the country would be green with envy to draw as well as our churches do in their combined congregations.

Now, say that only one-third—$33\frac{1}{3}$ percent—of the national population is in church on those Sunday mornings to hear Christ. How long do you estimate it will take before our Lord's ministry starts to have an impact on the North American church and then the society in general?

My guess is it wouldn't take long!

How tragic for the cause if those who minister the Word

can't fill this same role in the pulpit on Christ's behalf. It is a desperate day if the professionals have lost the ability to rally the troops as Jesus did, to again set them on fire, as always happens when revival touches the church.

Maybe it's time that all of us who preach begin regularly to examine ourselves to determine how well we are representing our Lord by speaking His thoughts. If Christ heard this Sunday's sermon, would He be pleased? As I see it, that's one of the burning questions of the day with which the clergy must grapple. Pastors should preach the same way they would were Christ Himself present in the church.

Oh, Jesus, please help those of us whom You have called to speak on Your behalf. Give us Your words and Your fire. Lord, have mercy upon our pitiful delivery of truth. Amen.

But another side must be examined as well—something also needs to be said to those who are hearers of the Word. Last Sunday in church, a man across the aisle from me and two pews ahead would have missed the miracle of what Jesus said had our Lord Himself come to preach. This attendee was asleep five minutes before the sermon began!

Others in church, though it's not as obvious to detect, habitually think about concerns at the office, or review the movie they saw on Saturday night, or anticipate the afternoon game they plan to watch on TV, or scan the mental list they've made of potential dates. It's a Sunday pattern, and as such it's extremely difficult (without laser lights and dancing ponies) to get through to these people with a simple sermon.

So let me continue my earlier sentence. Pastors should preach the Word *and parishioners should listen* the same way they would were Christ Himself present in the church. As simple as it sounds, this is another key measurement for determining how well a church is doing. When the Word is preached and heard, is it having a profound effect?

Have you ever invited an acquaintance to attend church with you, particularly someone who has been slightly critical of spiritual issues? Suddenly one's Sunday morning consciousness is excruciatingly heightened. You tend to observe everything that goes on—the singing, the preaching, the prayers, the offering—through the visitor's eyes and ears.

What's my friend thinking? you wonder. *Does he feel welcome? Will she want to come back?*

The same anticipatory awareness can be achieved through an experiment of inviting Christ to attend church as your guest for a few weeks.

This is a discipline I conduct almost every week. Since I'm no longer a pastor, but function in our church as a layman I invite Christ to be my guest, to go to church with my family. Some would call what I'm suggesting practicing the presence of Christ on Sunday morning. As with any visitor I bring, I attempt to consider His thinking more than my own.

This godly use of the imagination forces enormous attitudinal shifts upon me. "What time should we arrive at church?" becomes "Jesus, what time would You like for us to get there?"

I find myself asking, "Did the call to worship minister to You, my Lord? What about the congregational hymns? Did we sing them as though we meant them? Singing is not my long suit, but is there anything I can do to improve? When the Scriptures were read, did I give them the honor they deserve?"

And what about the sermon? I have trained my mind to listen to the sermon in the same attitude I would maintain were Christ seated bodily beside me. Before I consider my opinion as to its merit, I want to think through what I perceive as His response.

"Did the sermon do a good job of representing You, Jesus? Was the topic vital in Your mind, Christ? Do You believe it dealt with primary, pertinent issues or with secondary, superficial ones? Christ, did You pronounce, 'Amen'? Or were You disappointed, thinking it was a waste of time, simply a display of the speaker's thoughts but not of Your own? My Lord, did the message call for the kind of response You want from Your people? Am I right in thinking that You are still calling the church to awakening?"

Our opinion, our human evaluations—"I liked it!"; "The

illustrations were interesting"; "Appreciated the pastor's humor for a change"—these observations aren't nearly as important as whether or not we sense that the message had Christ's stamp of approval. Attempting to listen with Christ's ears will help us discern the level of a sermon's spiritual validity.

If week after week we feel Christ's disappointment, God help us. If nothing else, pray for a change; let us get down on our knees and plead for Holy Ghost power to return to the pulpit. Only then can we consider going to the pastor in love and sharing our concern.

The day demands it; time is running out. The consequences of impotent pulpiteers using words which aren't "en-Goded," which don't truly reflect Christ's thoughts, could result in family members' going to hell. This reality forces me to blunt communication—a powerless pulpit is a sign of insipid spirituality. And nationally, with our society's rush toward moral destruction, pulpit power becomes momentously imperative.

When God's people fail to take seriously the wonder of Christ's presence, when they treat the Holy Spirit with contempt, when they worship haphazardly, without awe, with no intellectual or emotional effort; by rote, ho-humming through the forms and not really caring what the minister says or doesn't say as long as he's halfway interesting—that's Ichabod all over again. The glory has departed.

So this Sunday extend an invitation. "Jesus, go to church with me as my guest." Listen through His ears. If you come away pleased, the authority of the sermon is only underscored, and you're doubly blessed.

If you come away disturbed, not for your own sake but for your Lord's, then at least go to your knees.

Pray like this: *"God, we desperately need a new sense of Your presence in our services. Show us how our church can be touched with spiritual fire. I plead with You to bring the sermons alive with power the way they would be were You to preach them Yourself. Amen."*

The Apostle Paul writes in 2 Cor. 2:17: "For we are not,

like so many, peddlers of God's Word; but as men of sincerity, as commissioned by God, in the sight of God we speak in Christ." Is this the way it is in your church? Or is the pastor simply presenting his thoughts about Scripture or the world in general? Each time he preaches, he should deliver a timely and vital truth on Christ's behalf. And those who listen should consider not only their response, but their Lord's as well—and obey what they know to be a Word from Him.

If Jesus is not with us in the church, all is for loss; the Scriptures are meaningless when they report that Christ is the acting head of His body, and success in the church—no matter the standard—is all an illusion.

But if Christ, by His Spirit, is truly present, shouldn't all of us—clergy and laity alike—make our number-one priority to see that He is pleased? And when this crucial awareness has been realized, our spiritual activity will be infused with the living Word—that which was from the very beginning, which was with God and was, in fact, God Himself.

For Discussion and Reflection

1. Do you recall a time when you were hungry for God's Word? What factors contributed to this appetite?

2. Fill in the blank. If it weren't for _____ , I would probably spend more time in God's Word.

3. Matthew 7:28 reads: "And when Jesus finished these sayings, the crowds were astonished at his teaching, for he taught them as one who had authority, and not as their scribes" (RSV).

   Would you say today's preaching is more in the style of Christ's or in the style of the scribes'? Why?

4. How would you prepare differently for church if Jesus were to preach this Sunday?

5. For revival preaching to be good, should it also be loud? Explain your answer.

Readings

IN REVIVAL, God's Word is seen to be truly dynamic. Hearts that have resisted the sermons and speeches of pastors and evangelists are suddenly broken by the hammer of the spirit. A phrase or a sentence from the Scriptures has broken down all resistance and brought the repentant heart to the feet of God for forgiveness and freedom.

In revival, God's Word is seen to be a Word speaking in definite terms to His people today. When God's Word is interpreted by cold-hearted hermeneutics, its basic meaning may, indeed, be given correctly, but its personal application is generally set aside. The interpreter claims he does not want to use the passage out of context or to misapply God's Word. But in times of revival, the Holy Spirit makes His own application of His Word to hearts. God's Word becomes His Word to me personally, definitely, directly.

—Ted S. Rendall, *Fire in the Church*, p. 30

— ◆ —

A GLIMPSE OF THE TRAVELS and preaching of George Whitefield in this country [in the mid-1700s] is given by a farmer of Middletown, Connecticut. He writes:

"Now it pleased God to send Mr. Whitefield into this land and my hearing of his preaching at Philadelphia like one of the old apostles. . . . I felt the spirit of God drawing me by conviction. I longed to see and hear him and wished he would come this way. . . . But next I heard he was on Long Island and next at Boston and next at Northampton, and then one morning all on a sudden about 8 or 9 o'clock, there came a messenger and said Mr. Whitefield preached at Hartford

and Wethersfield yesterday and is to preach at Middletown
this morning at 10 o'clock. I was in my field at work. I dropt
my tool that I had in my hand and ran home and ran through
the house and had my wife get ready quick to go and hear
Mr. Whitefield preach at Middletown and ran to my pasture
for my horse with all my might fearing I should be too late to
hear him. I brought my horse home and soon mounted and
took my wife up and went forward as fast as I thought the
horse could bear. . . . all this while fearing we should be
too late to hear the sermon for we had twelve miles to ride
double in little more than an hour and we went round by the
upper parish and when we came within half a mile of the
road that comes down from Hartford, Wethersfield, and
Stepney to Middletown on high land I saw before me a cloud
or fog rising, I first thought off from the Great River but as I
came nearer the road I heard a noise something like a low
rumbling thunder and I presently found it was the rumbling
of horses feet coming down the road, and this cloud was a
cloud of dust made by the running of horses feet, it arose
some rods into the air over the tops of the hills and trees and
when I came within about twenty rods of the road I could see
men and horses slipping along in the cloud like shadows and
when I came nearer it was like a steady stream of horses, and
their riders, scarcely a horse more than his length behind
another, all of a lather and foam with sweat, their breath
rolling out of their nostrils, in a cloud of dust every jump,
every horse seemed to go with all his might to carry his rider
to hear the news from Heaven to the saving of their souls. It
made me tremble to see the sight how the world was in a
struggle. I found a vacance between two horses to slip in my
horse and my wife said, 'Law, our clothes will be all spoiled,
see how they look'—for they was so covered with dust they
looked almost all of a color, coats and hats and shirts and
horses. We went down in the stream.

I heard no man speak a word all the way, three miles, but
every one pressing forward in great haste and when we got
down to the old meeting-house there was a great multitude,

it was said to be 3 or 4000 of people assembled together. We got off from our horses and shook off the dust and the ministers was then coming to the meeting-house. I turned and looked toward the Great River and saw the ferry boats running swift forward and backward bringing over loads of people, the oars rowed nimble and quick; everything, men, horses and boats seemed to be struggling for life; the land and the banks over the river looked black with people and horses. All along the twelve miles I see no man at work in his field but all seemed to be gone. When I see Mr. Whitefield come up upon the scaffold he looked almost angelical, a young slim slender youth before some thousands of people and with a bold undaunted countenance. And my hearing how God was with him everywhere as he came along it solemnized my mind and put me in a trembling fear before he began to preach for he looked as if he was clothed with authority from the great God and a sweet solemn Solemnity sat upon his brow, and my hearing him preach gave me a heart wound by God's blessing."

—Roland H. Bainton, *The Church of Our Fathers,* pp. 209–212.

BY THE SPIRIT Charles Finney became a man of prayer, and then quite spontaneously a preacher of the Gospel. He began witnessing and preaching in little school houses and country churches. In his *Memoirs* he recalled, "The Holy Spirit was upon me, and I felt confident that when the time came for action I should know what to preach. . . . The Spirit of God came upon me with such power, that it was like opening a battery upon them. For more than an hour, and perhaps for an hour and a half, the Word of God came through me to them in a manner that I could see was carrying all before it. . . . The Holy Spirit fell upon the congregation in a most remarkable manner. A large number of persons dropped their heads, and some groaned so that they could be heard throughout the house." Cataclysmic changes followed the powerful revival labors of Finney from the frontier areas of America to the British Isles.

—V. Raymond Edman, *They Found the Secret*, pp. 56–57

— ◆ —

NOWADAYS it is often said of D. L. Moody that he was not a student. I wish to say that he was a student; most emphatically he was a student. He was not a student of psychology; he was not a student of anthropology—I am very sure he would not have known what that word meant; he was not a student of biology; he was not a student of philosophy; he was not even a student of theology, in the technical sense of that term; but he was a student, a profound and practical student of the one Book that is more worth studying than all other books in the world put together; he was a student of the Bible. Every day of his life, I have reason for believing, he arose very early in the morning to study the Word of God, way down to the close of his life. Mr. Moody used to rise about four o'clock in the morning to study the Bible. He would say to me: "If I am going to get in any study, I have got to get up before the other folks get up"; and he would shut himself up in a remote room in his house, alone with his God and his Bible.

—R. A. Torrey, *Why God Used D. L. Moody*, pp. 20–21

— ◆ —

THE PROPHETS WERE a rare breed of men. They were God's emergency men for crisis hours. We need them at *this* hour in the history of America.

The prophets were God's Cabinet Members. He whispered His secrets to them. They shared His foreknowledge. Amos himself declares this amazing fact to be so. Hear him from chapter 3, verse 7 of his prophecy: "Surely the Lord God will do nothing, but he revealeth his secret unto his servants the prophets." . . .

Prophets differ from preachers. Preachers usually "make" sermons; prophets bring a message from the Lord. The prophet has no meticulous care about a sermon of homiletical perfection or of exigetical exactitude. His soul is aflame. He usually carries a death sentence and as such is a solemn soul. He does not scratch itching ears. He is out of step with the current preaching style. He usually shocks. . . .

Just a couple of days ago a fine preacher brother said to me, "We have no great preachers in the country anymore." I think I know what he meant: no outstanding man with a "thus saith the Lord," a man terrible in utterance under the anointing of the Spirit. We have gifted preachers, talented preachers, orator preachers, famous preachers, organizing preachers, but where, oh where, are the preachers *who startle the nation with prophetic utterance?* There is a famine of great preaching, a famine of strong expository preaching, a famine of conscience-stirring preaching, a famine of heartbreaking preaching, a famine of soul-tearing preaching, a famine of that preaching like our fathers knew which kept men awake all night lest they fall into hell. I repeat, "There is a famine of the word of the Lord."

—Leonard Ravenhill, *America Is Too Young to Die*, pp. 76–77, 79

7

Praying Boldly

— ◆ —

I T'S BEEN RIGHTLY OBSERVED that prayer is caught even more than it is taught. This was certainly true regarding the twelve apostles. They apparently felt they could learn quite a lot from their Lord after time and time again observing Him pray. What they had caught they now wanted to be taught, so they came to Christ and asked Him to give them instructions.

But what do people learn on Sundays through observing the prayer mannerisms in the church of our Lord?

Some might believe that God is far away or hard of hearing. That's because quite often the Sunday morning prayers are spoken LOUDLY and with exaggerated words and phrases.

Then again, someone else might conclude that the best and most proper prayers should always be carefully written out. Three-or-four-sentence liturgical prayers are best, they think, and they must always contain at least one "lofty" thought.

Repeated attendance at another church might convince some that only men should pray, or that true piety is indicated by the mastery of a certain droning vocal style accompanied by an occasional slight tonal waiver, or that exciting prayers always employ a vocabulary other than the common vernacular of the congregation, or that prayers go to heaven faster when organ music is played quietly in the background.

I have a conviction that to experience another day of awakening in the church, leaders are going to have to model what *boldness* in prayer is all about.

Boldness regarding prayer is mentioned frequently in the New Testament. And I'm convinced that boldness for the most part is lacking in the prayers of the church and desperately needs to be rediscovered. Never has there been revival without God's people learning the efficacy of prayer.

Let me share a few scriptures which make use of this same Greek word translated "boldness." Here's Ephesians 3:12: "In whom we have boldness and confidence of access through our faith in him." The same word *boldness* appears three times in Acts 4: "Now when they saw the boldness of Peter and John . . . they [the Jewish rulers, elders, and scribes] recognized that they had been with Jesus" (v. 13). "And now, Lord, look upon their threats, and grant to thy servants to speak thy word with all boldness" (v. 29). "And when they had prayed, the place in which they were gathered together was shaken; and they were all filled with the Holy Spirit and spoke the word of God with boldness" (v. 31).

In these Acts references the word relates primarily to a bold witness. But in Hebrews that same Greek word (here translated as "confidence") is used specifically regarding prayer: "Let us then with confidence [or boldness] draw near to the throne of grace" (Heb. 4:16).

The apostle John employs the word in his first Epistle: "Beloved, if our hearts do not condemn us, we have confidence [or boldness] before God; and we receive from him whatever we ask" (1 John 3:21). "And this is the confidence [or boldness] which we have in him, that if we ask anything according to his will he hears us" (1 John 5:14).

So boldness in prayer certainly means an increased confidence when talking to the Lord. The opposite would be a timidity in prayer, an uncertainty or a lack of faith that God will answer, or a basic doubt that He is even listening. And which description is more characteristic of the North American church today?

What about the prayers we model on Sunday mornings in our services? Do they manifest boldness (or confidence) in this vast spiritual resource that is ours? And will the cause of Christ move successfully forward in response to our typical timidity of expression, to our words spoken as though no one is listening, or to our coming into His presence with little forethought and relying on spiritual jargon and hackneyed phrases?

The church knows boldness when all its people pray exactly as though they were talking to Jesus face to face. The less Christians sense His presence, the less bold or confident they will be when they come before Him in prayer. This doesn't take the deductive reasoning of a genius to figure out; why put a lot into a conversation if you think the person you're talking to is not listening? Why be bold when your mind hasn't been captured by the majesty of the One to whom you have come to speak? The modeling of prayer in our worship services which is little more than verbalizations says to observing people, "Don't expect much, folks, because we don't really sense that the King is near enough to be responding at the moment."

The primary question this book asks is: What would happen if Jesus came in person and visited our churches? Even more specifically in this chapter, we're imagining how the life of the church would be transformed if we were all to actually hear Jesus say, "My subjects, I'm attentive and receptive right now to what you as a people have to say to Me."

All at once, would hands shoot up everywhere as people jockeyed with each other for His attention? Would believers start shouting requests: "Lord, Lord, over here . . ."? This might happen in a presidential press conference, but I don't believe people in the church would treat Christ this way. Because of the deep love and respect Christians have for this One whose name they bear, I rather suspect the time would begin with careful praise.

"How gracious of You, Lord, to grant us Your time and attention!"

"We're extremely fortunate, Your Majesty, to be Your people and to have You grace our church with Your presence."

"Lord Jesus, You have already done so much for us. Be aware that we hold Your name in deepest reverence."

Words like this are most fitting, and they prepare a congregation to come before the King with petitions appropriate to the corporate setting. They also teach parishioners volumes about the way we should talk to Christ when all alone.

If one person was chosen to speak this fitting praise on behalf of all, and then also to share the common concerns, what tone of voice should he or she use—loud, soft, normal?

Would the words be spoken quickly and spontaneously or more deliberately and chosen with care? Could written notes be used? Should the prayer sound efficient and businesslike or warmly personal? What posture might be assumed?

Once again, what we need always to be considering in response to questions such as these is: How would we talk to Christ were He before us in the flesh?

I don't pretend to have all the answers. But when leaders pray in our church services, I don't often sense that Christ's presence is perceived by them the way it should be or the way it is during times of revival in the church.

What if on Sunday morning our Lord interrupted the one praying the invocation or pastoral prayer and asked, "What is it actually, My friend, that you're attempting to say to Me?"

Would the person who has been praying know? Or have such prayers become verbal traditions which in reality merit little or no attention from Him? Might we not say, "Oh Jesus, I'm sorry; didn't You realize that these are just forms that meant something to someone somewhere, but not anymore? Don't bother Yourself; we're just going through the motions."

Often I also get a feeling, when people share their prayer requests, that they relate more to surface issues than to substantive ones. Seldom do the matters at hand touch in any way the deep concerns of the King who's being addressed. Instead, most of the requests expressed seem to center on the comfort of the subject voicing it.

Rarely do I hear this kind of statement: "Please look after this ailment, Jesus, so I can quickly return to the spiritual battle." More frequently, the attitude seems to be, "I don't like being sick, Jesus; can't You improve my lot in life?"

I believe the church must learn to refrain from voicing requests that would sound silly were the King bodily present to hear and to respond. Would some of us be in danger of actually hearing Christ say something like, "I understand that your house is in jeopardy of foreclosure. But this house has never once been used for the needs of My kingdom, so why should I grant this request? If the money is made available for the need, will that guarantee that this home will be used in some way for My holy cause? Has that thought ever been considered in terms of this request"?

If our prayers in church were actually spoken as though we were talking to Christ face to face, sooner or later a spiritual reality would begin to make itself known. This authenticity would then be caught by Sunday morning attendees and eventually make its way into the small prayer groups in the church as well as to individual prayer closets and private groanings before the Lord. God's people would rapidly begin to know a new and mighty confidence and boldness. When we realize that this is the King of the universe and that He has truly given us His attention, that realization results in boldness. And before we know it, we see early signs of revival. Revival and prayer always go together. They are inseparably linked.

Now, many people have trouble praying with confidence because they've never had an effective model for prayer. People are rightly suspicious when something doesn't work the way it should, when spiritual activities aren't all they're touted to be. And this is certainly true of prayer—if we've never seen results, we aren't going to be motivated to pray. But when expectations are achieved, when anticipations become actuality, intercessors quickly commit themselves to more and more prayer activity.

That's why the Twelve wanted Christ to teach them about prayer. It was obvious that prayer played a significant part in the life of their Master. His prayer life proved to be effectual. Reality in prayer, however, was not the experience of the Twelve. They didn't understand it all that much. Eventually prayer maturity would come, but at the moment, they, too— these followers, had lessons needing to be learned. I believe we, too, can benefit from what the Master taught them.

So in answer to His disciples' question in Luke 11:1, "Lord, teach us to pray," did Christ say "When you pray, say: Eternal and all powerful God, my top five wishes ranked in order of priority are as follows: (1) Sometimes being a Christian is lonely, so I want a close friend or companion; (2) I have a pain in the lower part of my back"?—well, hardly!

The truth is that Christ didn't instruct us to pray after the habit of many—"Here's my list of top requests for the week, God. Sorry I'm in such a hurry again." Rather, He said we are to emphasize the wonder of this face-to-face miracle that's ours by beginning, "Father." Christ couldn't have chosen a word that conveys more warmth or intimacy, could He?—*Father.* The very term in its most positive sense closes the distance we normally feel between ourselves and God.

According to Christ, then, effectual prayer begins with drawing close to God, or with this reminder of the divine nearness of the Father. That's because when we speak we need to be reminded that He is present, listening.

The Lord's short model prayer moves next to an expression of praise—"Hallowed be Thy name." These brief four words also speak volumes. They say, "Your very name is sacred. Though You've drawn near, I'm honored to be allowed here. I dare not rush into this privilege as though we were peers; I'm out of place if I do. Instead, as a lowly subject, I exalt in the wonder of who You are, Father; hallowed be Thy name." According to His Son, that's the way to talk to God when you want the conversation to manifest any reality.

"Thy kingdom come." This thought comes next. Why? It's a chief responsibility of ours to achieve empathy with the King's mind. We must learn to consider His concerns first, His kingdom and His kingship primarily. Yes, Lord, Your divine rule must be extended in my heart, my home, this church, this community, this nation. Thy kingdom come. And we must learn to do more than just repeat the words; we must liberate ourselves from pressing personal desires to re-say what the words mean and affirm that what they express is urgent in our hearts. As Alan Redpath has said, "Before we can pray, 'Lord, Thy Kingdom come,' we must be willing to pray, 'My kingdom go.'"

With Christ's kingdom in mind, we ask, "Lord, how are things going from Your perspective?" And because we're unpracticed at achieving this viewpoint in our prayers, it's important that we make a habit of anticipating his response. For instance, personalize his answer to this kingdom question:

"Christ, has Your reign benefited from the way I've been living? Have I pleased You by my actions? Advanced Your cause? Is the way God's will is being manifested in heaven also being modeled on earth by my lifestyle?" This is what is meant when we pray, "Thy kingdom come, thy will be done, on earth as it is in heaven" (Matt. 5:10).

After attempting to view activities from a kingdom perspective, Jesus then teaches us to talk about our needs for the given day: "Give us this day our daily bread" (v. 11). More generally, I believe this request means, "Please provide my necessities for this day, even as You promised You would if I'd seek Your kingdom first."

This is hardly a guarantee that someone in the congregation will win the state lottery or achieve a date with that special someone who makes the heart beat faster; nor does it insure the sale that will enable the purchase of that longed-for speed boat. This is not a surety that the exam will be passed (to which little study was devoted). No, Christ's statement about making requests reads simply, "Give us this day our daily bread." Restated it means, "Jesus please meet my needs for this day."

It's not necessary to cover all the teaching points of our Lord's prayer in order to conclude that the prayer pattern Christ taught His disciples resembles what we would follow if we spoke to Jesus face to face. Again, that's when I believe the church will begin to know boldness in prayer.

Some might think boldness means storming into heaven's courts, pushing everyone aside like a three-hundred-pound offensive tackle, demanding attention—"God, I'm here, ready to name it and claim it!"—and, during prayer, throwing around whatever spiritual clout you have—"I mean You don't have any choice, Lord. After all, I'm a big supporter of that Mains guy, the Chaplain in the Air (or whomever)!"

This is not boldness the way Christ taught it or modeled it.

Instead, boldness is the picture of a confident servant coming to his master in an attitude of praise ("Father, hallowed be Thy name"). The mindset is one of wanting most of all to serve the Lord well. Knowing God's will and doing it is the primary desire ("Thy kingdom come, my Lord; Thy will be done"). Of course, personal requests are also mentioned, but begging is not necessary; a simple statement of lack is all that is required. "Jesus, I need the following . . ." ("Give us this day our daily bread.")

"Lord, I'm bold to make this request. I see You granting it because it's in Your best interest, as well as enabling me to function most efficiently as Your servant." Now, that's a very different picture of boldness when compared to what most people have in mind; but the church will know this confidence the more it learns to think in terms of talking to Jesus face to face, remembering always who Christ is and who we are, the importance of His kingdom and the relative unimportance of our own little kingdoms, His promise to provide our needs and the insignificance of many of our wants, the reality of His presence even when we must see Him through eyes of faith.

How the church today languishes for this kind of praying. And in order for us to know success in this area, I believe huge adjustments need to be made. Fortunately, of all the measurements that indicate how much Christ's presence is perceived in the church, this is one of the easiest to evaluate and correct. I challenge all concerned Christians to examine their personal and corporate prayer lives in this light. And I challenge my fellow ministers and church lay leaders to begin to model what prayer is like for those in our spheres of influence. If we can't pray like Jesus did, can we not, at the very least, demonstrate for our people what it's like to talk to Him face to face?

It doesn't matter if the prayers in our services are long or short, written or spontaneous, personal or corporate; but we must make sure that those who do pray are aware that Christ is present, and listening to every word. It is urgently important that the prayers in our services not be allowed to be perfunctory.

I suspect that the way to begin correcting this problem is in the privacy of our own times alone with Christ. And again, whether it's the short session or the long season of prayer; whether you're coming before God with a notebook handy, with a list, or just with memory; whether you're kneeling, sitting, standing, or pacing—the question of importance is this: Are you conscious that Christ is there in the room with you, or are you just talking to the walls? Are you bold in prayer? Or have you just become adept at saying nice prayers, at reading them?

Lord, teach us to pray.

For Discussion and Reflection

1. Evaluate the prayer life of your church by what you can observe in the Sunday morning service.

2. If your personal prayer life was the standard for your local congregation, would revival be closer or farther off?

3. Are you more likely to pray consistently for revival by yourself or by becoming part of a small group committed to that purpose?

4. How does an increased awareness of Christ's presence make these parts of the prayer Christ taught His disciples more meaningful?

   ◆ Forgive us our debts, as we also forgive debtors.
   ◆ Lead us not into temptation, but deliver us from the evil one.

5. How could music be used more effectively during prayer times in worship services? Choral selections? Solos? Hymns? What might Christ's response be to your ideas?

Readings

SPEAKING ON ACTS 1:14, Dr. A. T. Pierson once said: "There never has been a revival but by such united supplicatory praying, and no revival has ever continued beyond the continuation of that same praying."

Most churches are said to fail because they do not generate their own power. This is also true of the individual Christian. Prayer is the generator. The great London preacher Charles Spurgeon once took some people down to his Metropolitan Tabernacle basement to show them his "power plant." There, on their knees, were about three hundred people praying for the service!

—Armin R. Gesswein, *With One Accord in One Place*, p. 21

— ◆ —

ON A BLEAK AND WINTRY DAY in 1794 twenty-three New England ministers sat down together to consider a problem that was pressing heavily upon them. They were disturbed about the spiritual condition of their country.

Here was the situation: The effects of the Great Awakening of 1735 had worn off. The seeds of infidelity, imported from revolutionary France and watered by such men as Thomas Paine, were yielding their poisonous fruit.

Eastern colleges were rife with the skepticism of the age. Lawlessness ruled on the western frontier. People were floundering in the bog of confusion created by the French and Indian War and the Revolution. There were few churches, few praying people. The established churches, most of whom had sided with England in the struggle for independence, had lost their influence.

The ministers were agreed on one thing—a revival was desperately needed.

"What shall we do about it?" they asked themselves. The only answer: pray.

They issued a "circular letter" calling on church people to pray for revival. They were specific. Let there be "public prayer and praise, accompanied with such instruction from God's Word, as might be judged proper, on every first Tuesday, of the four quarters of the year, beginning with the first Tuesday of January, 1795, at two o'clock in the afternoon . . . and so continuing from quarter to quarter, and from year to year, until, the good providence of God prospering our endeavors, we shall obtain the blessing for which we pray."

Apparently hearts were hungry, for there was an enthusiastic response.

All over the country little praying bands sprang up. In the West (Ohio, Kentucky, Tennessee) "Covenants" were entered into by Christian people to spend a whole day each month in prayer plus a half-hour every Saturday night and every Sunday morning.

Seminary students met to study the history of revivals. Church members formed "Aaron and Hur Societies" to "hold up the hands" of their ministers through intercession. Groups of young men went to their knees to pray for other young men. Parents prayed for their children's conversion.

The stage was set. What happened as a result of this concerted prayer effort has gone down as the most far-reaching revival in American history.

—*America's Great Revivals*, pp. 26–28

— ◆ —

IN MUCH OF THE CHURCH'S LIFE in the twentieth century, however, both in Evangelical and non-Evangelical circles, the place of prayer has become limited and almost vestigial. The proportion of horizontal communication that goes on in the church (in planning, arguing and expounding) is overwhelmingly greater than that which is vertical (in worship, thanksgiving, confession and intercession). Critically important committee meetings are begun and ended with formulary prayers, which are ritual obligations and not genuine expressions of dependence—when problems and arguments ensue, they are seldom resolved by further prayer but are wrangled out on the battlefield of human discourse. The old midweek prayer meetings for revival have vanished from the programs of most churches or have been transformed into Bible studies ending with minimal prayer. . . .

Part of the reluctance toward corporate prayer may stem from lack of practice in private prayer combined with a fleshly self-consciousness centered on the impression it is making rather than on the truth that God is hearing and answering. Or the reluctance to pray with others may reflect estrangement from them and unwillingness to settle disagreements and close the gap.

Beyond these expressions of the flesh there is a force in our minds resisting prayer like a solid barrier which must be broken. This force seizes on any and all of these good and bad excuses of the flesh and reinforces them in order to discourage us from praying. It is sometimes forgotten that if the devil can tempt us to do evil, he can also tempt us not to do good. He can glamorize sin, but he can also paint an ugly picture in our minds of any work which is the will of God, including prayer. Quietly and undetectably, he can embitter the image of prayer in our minds until we will unconsciously go out of our way to avoid it. The reason for this persistence on his part is obvious. It is adroitly summed up in the old couplet: "Satan trembles when he sees/The weakest saint upon his knees."

—Richard F. Lovelace, *Dynamics of Spiritual Life:*
An Evangelical Theory of Renewal, pp. 153, 155

— ◆ —

IN CHICAGO, [1857–58] where 2,000 showed up for prayer in the Metropolitan Theater, a newspaper commented: "So far as the effects of the present religious movement are concerned, they are apparent to all. They are to be seen in every walk of life, to be felt in every phase of society. The merchant, the farmer, the mechanic—all who have been within their influence—have been incited to better things; to a more orderly and honest way of life. All have been more or less influenced by this excitement."

And everywhere, it was a revival of prayer. There was no hysteria, no unusual disturbances. Just prayer.

Finney said: "There is such a general confidence in the prevalence of prayer, that the people very extensively seemed to prefer meeting for prayer to meeting for preaching. The general impression seemed to be, 'We have had instruction until we are hardened; it is time for us to pray.'"

In a church in the Midwest twenty-five women got together once a week to pray for their unconverted husbands. The pastor traveled to the Fulton Street meeting to testify that on the Sunday he had left the last of the twenty-five husbands had been received into the church.

At the very first union prayer meeting held in Kalamazoo, Michigan, someone put in this request: "A praying wife requests the prayers of this meeting for her unconverted husband, that he may be converted and made an humble disciple of the Lord Jesus."

At once a stout, burly man arose and said, "I am that man. I have a pious, praying wife, and this request must be for me. I want you to pray for me."

As soon as he sat down, another man got up and said, "I am that man. I have a praying wife. She prays for me. And now she asked you to pray for me. I am sure I am that man, and I want you to pray for me."

Three, four or five or more arose and said, "We want you to pray for us too." That started a revival that brought at least 500 conversions.

—America's Great Revivals, pp. 64–66

— ◆ —

MY HEART WAS STIRRED, my spiritual pulse quickened, when I talked privately with Duncan Campbell, so used of the Lord in what is called the Hebrides Revival. In this small group of islands off the west coast of Scotland is a place called Barvas, a village on the island of Lewis and Harris. Campbell was asked to preach there, but he could not go; he was already committed to other places. There had been powerful prayer ascending to the throne for a move of the Spirit in the place. Not the least of the intercessors, indeed some would say the most powerful of them, were two sisters, Peggy and Christine Smith. They were eighty-four and eighty-two years old respectively and spoke only Gaelic. Peggy was blind and her sister almost bent double with arthritis ("God hath chosen the weak things of the world to confound the things which are mighty"—1 Cor. 1:27).

Faith comes by hearing. These precious intercessors had grasped the promise, "I will pour water upon him that is thirsty, and floods upon the dry ground" (Isa. 44:3). This they pleaded day and night in prayer. Campbell's refusal to go to Barvas was accepted as the mind of the Lord, at least by most folks. However, Peggy, the blind prayer warrior, would have none of it. She had the promise. Her spirit, if not her voice, was saying, "I will not let Thee go until Thou bless Barvas!"

The second letter saying that Duncan Campbell could not come to the place brought this answer from her: "That's what the *man* says —*God* has said otherwise! Write again! He will be here within a fortnight [two weeks]." He went!

After Campbell had preached on the foolish virgins and come down from the pulpit, a young deacon raised his hand and, moving it in a circle over his head, said, "Mr. Campbell, God is hovering over. He is going to break through. I can hear already the rumbling of heaven's chariot wheels."

The entire congregation was lingering outside the church. Many faces showed signs of deep spiritual distress. Suddenly a young man, overburdened for the lost around him, broke out in an agonizing cry—his prayer was aflame! So overcome was he that he fell into a trance and lay prostrate on the floor. The congregation moved back into the church. Many sought the Lord. There was great grief over and repentance for sin. Now the revival was on!

While the Lord was working in the church building, Peggy and her sister were interceding at the throne. Peggy sent the following message to her minister—listen to this language, not common to our ears used to all our mass evangelism and flamboyant gospel shows:

> We struggled through the hours of the night, refusing to take a denial. Had He not promised, and would He not fulfill? Our God is a covenant-keeping God, and He must be true to his covenant engagements. Did He fail us? Never! Before the morning light broke, we *saw* the enemy retreating, and our wonderful Lamb take the field.

When asked what supported their faith in the prayer encounter, Peggy answered, "We had a consciousness of God that created a confidence in our souls which refused to accept defeat."

Yes, there is a word that says, "Touch not mine anointed, and do my prophets no harm" (1 Chron. 16:22). But what if the prophet is temporarily out of hearing of the Lord? Andrew Woolsey, the biographer of Duncan Campbell, talked of Peggy's having a holy intimacy with the Lord. How right he is. Paul said, "I withstood [Peter] to the face, because he was to be blamed" (Gal. 2:11). Peggy withstood Campbell. She had asked the preacher to come to a small, isolated village and hold a meeting. The people of that village were not in favor of the revival-type meetings. Duncan told Peggy so, and that he doubted her wisdom in this thing. She turned in the direction of his voice, her sightless eyes seeming to penetrate his soul, and said, "Mr. Campbell, if you were living as near to God as you ought to be, He would reveal His secrets to you, also."

Duncan accepted the rebuke. Then he knelt with Peggy, and the dear intercessor said, "Lord, You remember what You told me this morning, that in this village You are going to save seven men who will be pillars in the church of my fathers. Lord, I have given Your message to Mr. Campbell, and he seems not prepared to accept it. O Lord, give him wisdom, because he badly needs it."

Duncan went to the village, preaching in the large room of a house. His message was, "The times of this ignorance God winked at; but now commandeth all men everywhere to repent" (Acts 17:30). By the time he was through preaching, many were mourning for their sins—among them, Peggy's seven men!

—Leonard Ravenhill, *Revival: God's Way,* pp. 102–104

8

Got to Tell Somebody

— ◆ —

GOOD NEWS IS HARD to keep to yourself for very long. The other Monday when my secretary walked into my office I knew something was up because there was a big smile on her face. Before she said a word I had it figured out. The young man standing next to her had proposed that last weekend.

This same dynamic is true about good news shared by many. Being a sports fan from Chicago, I will admit the news hasn't been good all that often. But when the Bears or the Cubs are winning, the whole city is caught up in the excitement. That's because good news is fun to talk about.

And I can't think of any news that would thrill me more than to hear that church people throughout the United States and the provinces of Canada were sharing good news with others about fresh encounters with the living Christ.

If Jesus actually could be seen in His resurrected body, wouldn't that be something? Add a miracle or two, maybe a healing of someone who's been crippled, and it's "Katy bar the door!" There will not be a stadium large enough to hold everyone who's interested in this kind of good news.

Were you aware that times of genuine revival are exactly like this? During revival Christ's followers are convinced of the reality of their Lord's involvement in their lives, and they can't keep from telling others about it.

Is this unfamiliar territory for you? Then allow me to remind you that it is *orthodox* for a Christian to believe that Christ is present whenever two or three gather in His name. We believe this in our heads because Jesus Himself said it was true. The problem is that often the reality of what the Lord declared is not experienced in a meaningful way. Consequently, the gospel, or the good news, ceases to be the talk of the town.

The Presbyterian revivalist Charles Finney, whose writings move me greatly, declared that when people in the church are no longer interested in telling others about Christ, something is basically wrong with their faith. His pragmatic diagnosis concluded that such congregations are in a back-slidden state. If I understand Finney correctly, whopping big attendance records, new educational wings constructed right and left, graded choir programs, and Christian aerobic classes still mean relatively little if only a handful in the church have any interest in non-Christians' meeting Jesus. What would Christ Himself say about a "booming" church which for some strange reason showed no interest in bringing others to meet Him?

One way to correct this problem is by creating programs designed to train people to witness, evangelize, win souls, pass out tracts, and so on. And while there can be value in these methods, we must realize that their success will be only temporary if the excitement quotient regarding Christ is not high. What really motivates people to tell others about the church is not involvement in an evangelism program but the conviction that the living Christ is truly with us and miraculously changing us.

That's why I believe it is wise for congregations to concentrate first on welcoming Christ into all aspects of the life of the Body. The members need to go out of their way to do by faith what they know pleases their Lord and makes Him most comfortable. Once a church is convinced of Christ's presence, her people want to tell others their exciting news.

What spread the faith like wildfire in those early centuries of the church? Was it "You have to come, we have programs for everyone" or "You have to come; our pastor is a spellbinding preacher" or "You have to come, it's a great congregation"? No, I believe what those early Christians said was, "You need to meet the One called Jesus. He's God's Son, and He'll change your life! Come and see!"

Christ's perceived presence makes a qualitative difference in how we view the spiritual life of a church. When it is clear to all that Christ is present, we work on truly worshiping Him. As Christ insisted, we love not only Him, but our brothers and sisters as well. Walking righteously becomes extremely important because of its great importance to our Lord, who came to destroy the works of the devil. Conscious of the King's presence, we as loyal subjects think more in terms of service than of being served. We listen to His word as though Jesus Himself were physically near. We set aside quality time to talk with Him face to face in prayer.

Christ then honors such efforts to please Him by the further revelation of Himself—not physically through His resurrected body, but in a very real way nevertheless, through His Spirit. The church begins to experience an increased infilling of His peace, His joy, His oneness, His strength, His beauty . . . and in the naturalness and excitement of it all, it also knows numerical growth.

Admittedly, this approach differs from that to which we're usually accustomed. Today we think, "Concentrate on evangelism. Get the message out, that's what's all important! What's going on in the church is secondary. Even if it's backslidden, we can still evangelize."

But old-time revivalists like Finney thought differently. They emphasized renewing the church first. If the church falls in love with Christ again, if the people of God start experiencing the dynamics of what church life is supposed to be, if the marvelous presence of Jesus is again experienced, there will be such an excitement and attractiveness to what's happening that evangelism will fall into place.

Such thinking didn't mean that reaching out to nonbelievers was deemphasized. No, just the opposite was true; if anything, evangelism received a greater emphasis. But then, during revival, it was easier to talk to others about the value of something that was working in believers' lives. This spontaneous enthusiasm stands in vivid contrast to an effort mounted to motivate Christians to sell others on a kind of Christianity that works on an intellectual basis, but seems to be limping along in actual experience.

"Besides," said these spiritual movers and doers from earlier generations, "bringing new Christians into a backslidden church is counter-productive." I think they had a point. Defining his position in the classic book, *Revival Lectures,*

Finney wrote, "While Christians are in their backslidden state, they are blind to the state of sinners. But when there is revival . . . they will feel grieved that others do not love God when they love Him so much. They will not only be urging them to give their hearts to God, but they will carry them to God in the arms of faith, and with strong crying and tears beseech God to have mercy on them."[1] According to Finney, if revival is emphasized, evangelism will be the natural outgrowth.

No one wants to be a hypocrite. Maybe you once experienced Christ and know that you belong to Him. But if you're not living for Him, if He doesn't seem as close today as He did at your conversion, if the glow is gone, you'll naturally not speak about Him to others as frequently as you once did. But when you're near to Christ, truly living close to Him; when you're aware of God's Son changing you into the person He wants you to be; when you're filled with His Spirit and marked more and more with the fruits of love, joy, peace, patience, kindness, goodness, faithfulness, gentleness, self-control . . . well, it's going to be practically impossible not to share with others what Christ has done and is doing!

Multiplied many times over, that dynamic will be true of the whole church. If the reality of Christ's presence is missing, the natural witness of the church diminishes. If Christ's reality overwhelms a congregation, that good news will be enthusiastically shared. Spontaneous evangelism is as simple as that.

I long for that day in the church when once again God's people are excited about the Lord and His ministry among them, when families learn to love one another and spouses are reconciled, when neighbors put aside old grievances, when guilt and shame are released through repentance and forgiveness, when healings occur because of a growing atmosphere of belief, when the alcoholic and drug addict are freed from substance abuse, when joy comes tumbling into the depression of lives and the whistle returns, when the outcast is made to feel at home, when the lonely find a caring community, when children grow up to love and serve God, when people are eager to attend church and Sunday is the high point of the week.

When Christ was here on earth, He generated tremendous excitement wherever He went. Scriptural incidents are mostly recorded without emotional elaborations; the missing details and the built-in drama are left to the readers' imaginations. This is certainly true of the story of Jairus' daughter, which is found in three of the four gospels (Matt. 9, Mark 5, and Luke 8): "And there came a man named Jairus, who was a ruler of the synagogue; and falling at Jesus' feet he besought him to come to his house, for he had an only daughter, about twelve years of age, and she was dying" (Luke 8:41–42).

That is the bare-bones account. But so much is there between the lines. Christian recording artist Don Francisco, in one of his best-selling recordings, captures this drama of that story as he assumes the role of Jairus:

> We were still a long way down the road when I heard the
>   sounds and cries,
> Of the mourners and musicians as they strove to dramatize
> My grief they had no business with beneath their loud disguise.
> My wife just sat there silently and stared through empty eyes.
>
> Then Jesus asked the mourners, why is it that you weep?
> She isn't dead as you supposed, the child is just asleep.
> It only took a moment for their wails to turn to jeers:
> "Who does this man think he is? Get him out of here."[2]

The child, of course, is raised from the dead. Luke 8:56 reads that Jesus "charged them to tell no one what had happened." Yet again Don Francisco captures so well the emotion of that moment:

> Then he called his three disciples that were with him on the way.
> He led them and my wife and me to where our daughter lay.
> He took her by the hand, he told her, "Child arise."
> And the words were barely spoken when she opened up
>   her eyes.

149

She rose and walked across the room and stood there at our sides.
My wife knelt down and held her close and at last she really cried.
Then Jesus told us both to see our daughter had some food;
And as to her, how her life was saved, not to speak a word.[3]

Then there's a long pause in the song, an interlude in the melody line, almost as though the story has come to an end. But no, quietly the words begin again: *I got to tell somebody. I got to tell somebody.*

And the line repeats itself with conviction and crescendo: I got to tell somebody! I got to tell somebody! Over and over the desire is sung:

> I got to tell somebody!
> I got to tell somebody what Jesus did for me.
> You know he gave me life when our hope was dead.
> When there was grief he brought joy instead.
> I got to tell somebody!
> I got to tell somebody!
> I got to tell somebody what Jesus did for me.[4]

What an incredible account! Why did Christ impose this silence on parents whose joy was overbounding? What a tremendous favor—the reviving of a precious daughter, life returning for one you hold most dear. Impossible silence, to be told, "Don't speak a word of this to anyone."

But maybe that's what Christ should have imposed upon some of us to whom He's given the gift of spiritual life. Perhaps He should have instructed us: Don't dare say a word! Then we might appreciate more the privilege of sharing.

What is wrong with the church today? The great percentage of those who attend week after week have always been there (or have transferred to this congregation from another). Where are the new people? Those who hurt? The ones feeling constant dread, depression, discouragement? Are there no more who stare through empty eyes?

If Christ is in the church Sunday after Sunday, as He promised and as we affirm through our understanding of doctrine, why are so few pressing in to touch Him or cupping their hands to call out His name?

If others don't know where to find Christ, why aren't those of us who regularly attend church bringing friends to meet Him?

"But you don't know our church!" someone shouts. "Finding Jesus in our services is like looking for the proverbial needle in the haystack. Our preacher doesn't even believe in Christ's divinity."

How right a common complaint like this—and if this is so, why aren't we on our knees pleading, weeping, longing for sweeping spiritual regenesis?

I know I'm a broken record, but in times of revival it's Christians who are grieved over the lostness of those they love who make a difference. Wives pray for their husbands, fathers for their sons, daughters for their mothers, neighbors for neighbors. They want to see others come to Jesus; they want to see others come to Jesus; they want to see others come to Jesus—there, I moved the needle. But did you catch the message?

I deeply believe it is time to return to basics, to spiritual life in the church that generates from and runs parallel to that of the New Testament, where the Good News of Christ was really good news. That seems to me a better route, a more honest approach, than redefining church success according to human standards so we won't look bad. ("Take a peek at these new floor plans. We even have a gym for the kids—and in a couple of years we can add a swimming pool.")

"Good news refreshes the bones" (Prov. 15:30). Don't the dry bones of God's people today need refreshing?

"O Sovereign Lord, you alone know," cried Ezekiel when the Spirit showed him the valley full of bones.

He led me back and forth among them, and I saw a great many bones on the floor of the valley, bones that were very dry. He asked me, "Son of man, can these bones live?"

I said, "O Sovereign Lord, you alone know."

Then he said to me, "Prophesy to these bones and say to them, 'Dry bones, hear the word of the Lord!' . . ."

So I prophesied as I was commanded. And as I was proph-
esying, there was a noise, a rattling sound, and the bones came
together, bone to bone. I looked, and tendons and flesh appeared on them and skin covered them, but there was no breath
in them.

Then he said to me, "Prophesy to the breath; prophesy, son
of man, and say to it, . . . 'This is what the Sovereign Lord
says: O my people. . . . I will put my Spirit in you and you
will live . . . Then you will know that I the Lord have spoken,
and I have done it, declares the Lord'" (Ezekiel 37:2–14, NIV).

What a great prophecy to be given! What a great prophecy
to give! Good news! Life's coming again to this dry valley of
death!

Life coming back again. That is what revival is all about.

Think about the word itself. V-I-V words relate to life:
vivid means full of life; a *vivacious* person is lively; *viva!*
means "to life!" The prefix *re* means again, so *reviv* means life
coming back again. The suffix *al* is "that which pertains to."
So *revival* is that which pertains to life coming back
again . . . even to church—or a nation—that's like a valley
of dry bones.

Good news from God is hard to keep to yourself.

I got to tell somebody!

For Discussion and Reflection

1. Name some people you know in your church who have become Christians in the past year.

2. If asked to teach a Sunday School class on the topic of "How to pray for your non-Christian friends," what would you share?

3. Which would influence you more in the direction of inviting others to church and why?

   ◆ A proven program on "How to Witness."
   ◆ An increased awareness of Christ's presence in the services.

4. If a person doesn't have exceptional verbal skills, are there other ways to share one's Christian faith? Give specific examples.

5. How would you react to this announcement in the Sunday church bulletin?

   In three months there will be a revival in our church. Begin now making a list of unsaved friends you will want to invite.

Readings

ANY CHURCH that is discovering the thrill of revival
will . . . be actively seeking to win the lost. Revival and
evangelism, though different in nature, issue from the same
source and flow together. It is true that a passion for souls is
one fruit of revival, but it is also apparent that this love
grows as we become involved in the work. A church which
does not go out into the world to press the claims of the
Kingdom would not know revival if it came.

Evangelism might be called the spiritual thermometer of
the Church. When the body of believers is sick, the evangelistic program is usually the first thing to stagger. Custom
and pride will keep other programs going long after their
purpose is lost. Yet that part of the church activity which is
not expressing the Saviour's love for lost men is simply out
of touch with the Gospel. How tragic it is when the concern
for fellowship, civic improvement, intellectual attainment,
social welfare or some other secondary consideration, becomes the controlling passion of church life.

This confusion of priorities is doubtless one of the most
bewildering problems confronting the Christian community.
It is not easy to keep first things first in the Church, but it is
even harder to face the consequences of not doing so. The
harsh truth is that whenever evangelism is relegated to an
incidental place in a church's program, the church begins to
die, and unless something happens to reverse the trend,
eventually the church will become extinct. The Church can
continue only as the people of God reproduce their life in
each succeeding generation.

This does not happen by accident. We must aim at the
target to hit it. The sentimental idea that somehow evangelism will take care of itself provided we live a good life has a
subtle way of beguiling us to sleep. On the other hand, a
constant whirl of activity in the church is no assurance that

people are being converted. Crowds may come to the Sunday services, large building programs may be completed, big budgets may be raised, tremendous energy may be expended in many worthwhile things—and evangelism may still be missing. Making Christ known and loved must become a commitment of life.

—Ronald E. Coleman, *Dry Bones Can Live Again:*
Revival in the Local Church, pp. 82–83

— ◆ —

AS THE ENGLISH CHURCH had been in need of revival in Wesley's day, so a century later Methodism itself was in need of revival. The great-grandchildren of the first poor Methodists had grown too prosperous to care greatly for the poor of their own day. Yet the Methodist Church still had enough of the spirit of Wesley to make more men who were like him. One was William Booth, the founder of the Salvation Army. . . . As Wesley went to England's poor at the mouths of the coal pits, Booth found them in London's slums. As Wesley used boulders for pulpits, Booth used curbstones. The Methodist leaders called Booth to a conference and told him that he must settle in a church and give only half his time to the poor. His wife Catherine, who was there, called to him: "Never, William! Never!"

Together they started a movement after Wesley's own heart. And they did more than preach to the poor. They started soup kitchens, shelters for the men sleeping on the bridges, homes for girls in trouble. And Booth woke up all England by a book called *In Darkest England.* A book had just come out with the title *In Darkest Africa.* Booth showed that England was darker still.

As Wesley had taken lay preachers, so Booth took those who were won and put them right to work winning others. Zeal mattered more than book learning. Once a fisherman was preaching on the story of Jesus in which the servant said to his master, "Lord, I feared thee because thou art an austere man." The fisherman thought it was "oyster man," and told how the oyster fishermen had to get wet and dirty and cut their hands on the shells to win the oysters. So Jesus suffered to win men. Twelve men were won that night, and when the mistake was pointed out to the fisherman, he said: "Never mind! We got twelve oysters."

—Roland H. Bainton, *The Church of Our Fathers*, pp. 196–197

— ◆ —

[REPORT OF Rev. Dr. B. T. Kavanaugh, who served in the South during the Civil War:]

"I obtained leave of absence and made my escape by riding all night alone, and found myself outside of Grant's lines the next morning, and went into Selma, Ala., where I spent the summer. I requested Bishop Paine to give me a commission as a missionary to Gen. Price's army, which was then in Arkansas. . . .

"My first work was to organize all the chaplains and missionaries into an Association for mutual aid and cooperation. When we went into camp at Camp Bragg, 30 miles west of Camden, we there commenced our work in earnest. Through the winter of 1863–'64 we kept up our meetings in camp, had seats and pulpit prepared, and were successful in having more than one hundred conversions.

"After the battles of Mansfield and Pleasant Hill, in Louisiana, our armies returned to Arkansas and made an encampment at a place called Three-Creeks, on the southern line of the State of Arkansas. Here I commenced preaching on the 10th of June, 1864, and continued our meetings until the 10th of September. An extensive revival commenced within a few days after our meeting commenced, and grew in interest and power to the close. We had preaching, beginning at early candle-light—or rather pine-knot fires on stands around the preaching-place. After about ten o'clock at night, the preaching and other exercises at the stand closed; but this was but the beginning of the night's work.

"As soon as dismissed, the young converts gathered in groups of tens and twenties, and went off in companies into the adjoining woods; and taking their friends, penitents seeking religion, with them, they spent the whole night in singing, praying, and praising God. I had lodgings close by the camp at Mrs. Tooke's, a sister of Gen. Buckner, from which, night after night, at all hours, until morning, I could hear the shouts of the new-born souls and the rejoicing of those who were laboring with them for their salvation. . . .

"The people in the country around us became interested in our meetings, and attended them. The remark had been made by many, before our revival meetings commenced, that it was very difficult for a man to be religious in the army; but now it was far more common to hear it said that no one could be very religious unless he belonged to the army.

"Like meetings were held in other camps of the same army at some ten, twenty, and thirty miles from us. . . .

"To show the genuineness of this work of grace upon the lives of these converts, we have to remark that after our camp was broken up, and the army was put upon the march to distant fields, wherever we went into camp but for a night our boys held prayer-meetings every night, greatly to the astonishment of the people in the country who were witnesses of their devotion.

"After the army was disbanded, in riding through the country in Arkansas and Texas, I met with some of our converts, who had returned to their families and parents, and they were still true to their profession and evinced a decidedly firm Christian character.

"The parents of some of those young men have since told me that in place of having the characters and habits of their sons ruined by being in the army they had returned to them as happy Christian men." . . .

Up to January, 1865, it was estimated that nearly *one*

hundred and fifty thousand soldiers had been converted during the progress of the war, and it was believed that fully one-third of all the soldiers in the field were praying men and members of some branch of the Christian Church. A large proportion of the higher officers were men of faith and prayer, and many others, though not professedly religious, were moral and respectful to all the religious services and confessed the value of the revival in promoting the efficiency of the army.

—William W. Bennett, *The Great Revival Which Prevailed in the Southern Armies During the Late Civil War Between the States of the Federal Union,* pp. 347–49, 413

— ◆ —

[WILLIAM P. NICHOLSON, an Irish Evangelist converted during the English revivals in the early 1900s, tells his story:]

"The fear of man was a dreadful snare, and I was helplessly caught by it. I was ashamed of Christ, and ashamed of being seen with out-and-out Christians. I was a sneak and a coward, if ever there was one. I despised myself, but was helpless about it. . . .

"The Salvation army had come to our town. The Corps was composed of two wee girls in uniform. They held open-air meetings and made a noise with their tambourines. Their first soldier was a man called Daft Jimmy. He had hardly enough brains to give him a headache, but he had sense enough to get saved. He carried the flag as they marched the streets. On his jersey, a red one, he had the women put with white yarn these words on his back, 'Saved from public opinion.'

"I was told by Satan that I would have to go to the open-air meeting and march down the street with two wee girls and a fool. . . . I would be laughed at by all my friends. I would lose my reputation.

"I said, 'Lord, I will be willing to go to Timbuctoo or Hong Kong, or even die decently as a martyr.' I couldn't get out of it. I became more and more miserable and, oh, so hungry for freedom and victory.

"At last I became desperate. The last night of the convention I saw it was a clean-cut, unconditional surrender; or continued wandering in failure, defeat and dissatisfaction. I left the meeting and went down to the shore, and there under a clear sky and shining stars I made the complete unconditional surrender. I cried out, 'Come in. Come in, Holy Spirit. Thy work of great blessing begin. By faith I lay hold of the promise, and claim complete victory over sin.'

"Hallelujah! What a thrill, what a peace, what a joy! Although an old-fashioned Presbyterian I began to weep and sing and rejoice like an old-fashioned Free Methodist. . . .

"As I walked down the street that Saturday it seemed as if every friend and relative I ever had were out and about. When I came to the open-air meeting and saw the two wee Salvation Army girls singing and rattling their tambourines, and poor Daft Jimmy holding the flag, I nearly turned back. Talk about dying! I was dying hard that night. I stepped off the footpath, and stood in the ring. The soldier looked at me. Then to my horror one of them said, 'The people don't stop and listen: let us get down on our knees and pray.' What could I do? I couldn't run away. So down I got on my knees.

"The crowd gathered around. I could hear their laughter and jeers. The officer prayed a telegram prayer—short and to the point. I could have wished the prayer had been as long as the 119th Psalm. I stood up, blushing and nervous. They got the collection while the crowd was there, and then to my horror, she said, 'Brother! take this tambourine and lead the march down the street to the Barracks.' I couldn't let a girl beat me, so I took it. That did it. My shackles fell off, and I was free; my fears all gone.

"I started down the street, whether in the body or out of the body, I can't tell. I lost my reputation, and fear of man: joy and peace and glory filled me. I can see now, and understand why the Lord dealt with me so drastically. I would never, I believe, have come right through and out-and-out for

Christ, in any other way. I was naturally timid and shy. I lost something that night I never want to find again, and I found something I never want to lose. That is, I lost my reputation and fear of man, and found the joy and peace of the over-flowing fullness of the Spirit. Hallelujah!"

On street corners and in cottages, in the city and in the villages, in his place of employment on the railroad and in the churches, Nicholson became a fearless and flaming winner of souls.

—V. Raymond Edman, *They Found the Secret: Twenty Transformed Lives That Reveal a Touch of Eternity*, pp. 107–110

— ◆ —

SINCE THE REVIVAL'S BEGINNING, [Asbury College and Seminary, 1970] thousands of people have become involved in various kinds of redemptive ministry. Some visit homes for the aged; some work with delinquents and school dropouts; some are becoming more active in community affairs. One day scores of seminary students went out to clean up a garbage dump, sweep the streets, and paint a widow's house.

Most impressive has been the way people have fanned out across the nation to share their testimony. Some weekends as many as two-thirds of the Asbury student body were away on these witness excursions. Where they have gone, others have caught the vision. By now a veritable army of people have seen God use them in this way.

To a remarkable degree, the revival has given practical substance to the New Testament concept of the priesthood of all believers. Distinctions between clergy and laity have all but vanished. People are learning as never before that they can and must minister as servants of Christ.

Usually they are not gifted speakers; nor are they especially well trained in methods of evangelism. Yet people marvel at their ability to communicate. The sincerity and earnestness of their approach command respect. They know whereof they speak, and they are not afraid to say it. As one witness boldly affirmed, "I feel like Paul walking into a city with the message of God."

—Harold Spann, Assistant to the President, Asbury College, writing in *One Divine Moment*, pp. 98–99

9

The Best of Times

— ◆ —

WHEN THE CHURCH is functioning at its best, when it's on fire for the Lord, the presence of Christ is the focus of corporate life. In such a church, it's not the building of which the people are most proud. The pastor isn't the personality whose name dominates all conversations. The denominational program isn't what's pushed most. It is *Christ* who is the center of interest.

Overly idealistic? Travel back in your mind to the early church. What excited the people then? It was Christ, Christ and His kingdom, Christ and His kingship.

I don't want to be impossibly naïve about the first-century church. First Corinthians reveals how the believers quarreled about being disciples of Apollos or Cephas or Paul. But the apostle chided them: "Let's end this right now. Is Christ divided? Was Paul crucified for you?"

Maybe they were more like us back then than we want to know. Even with Paul's strong affirmation that Jesus was the one crucified, the only one who could forgive sin, with passing years, Christ's importance began to fade. And too often in the dimming light of forgetfulness matters such as

- learning the "deeper things" of the faith
- holding conventions on doctrinal purity
- building cathedrals and parish churches
- experiencing "in depth" fellowship
- resolving church/state issues
- developing religious forms for the masses
- trying heretics
- raising funds to meet great budgets
- going on crusades
- establishing schools for clergy
- opening up the religious arts
- fighting church politics

165

- solving male/female roles
- getting involved in social issues
- participating in intrachurch bowling leagues
- pledging allegiances to various religious media ministries

started occupying front and center attention. Eventually, in such situations, Christ just wasn't talked about or thought about that much. Far too often, church history involves a discouraging downward spiral of spiritual life that has been expressed in repetitive cycles.

But this is true also: during the best of times, the years when the spiritual fire burned most brightly, the presence of Christ was the dominant feature. While judging current success in our churches, we do well to compare ourselves not to other churches, but to times when there was this overwhelming sense of divine spiritual presence.

Though Jesus was not physically present, His people acted as though He had visited them bodily:

- They *worshiped* Him.
- They were careful to show Christlike *love* to one another, as He commanded.
- They scrupulously avoided His archenemy, Satan, and shunned all that the evil one stood for. They were a *holy* people.
- They *served* Christ with gladness and self-sacrifice, considering this a great privilege.
- They paid close attention to what He said in *Scripture* and through the spoken word—and they obeyed what they read and heard.
- They spent quality time talking to Him in *prayer*.
- They *told their friends* about Him.
- They felt that, regarding the church, these were the *best times possible* to be living.

Let me give an illustration. Most historians would say that the first fifty years of colonial life in our land were characterized by deep earnestness and spiritual passion. By the beginning of the 1700s, however, the fires of religious fervor had begun to die.

In 1721, Dr. Increase Mather, a Puritan pastor and former president of Harvard University, penned these sad words:

> I am now in my eighty-third year, and having been for sixty-five years a preacher of the gospel, I cannot but be in the disposition of those ancient men who had seen the foundation of the first house, and wept with a loud voice to see what a change the temple had upon it. The children of New England are, or once were, the children of godly men. What did our fathers come into this wilderness for? Not to gain estates, as men do now, but for religion, and that they might leave their children in a hopeful way of being truly religious. Oh, degenerate new England, what are thou come to at this day? How art those sins become common in thee that were once not so much as heard of in this land?[1]

Thankfully, the darkness about which Mather wrote proved to be that which preceded the dawn. In 1734, Jonathan Edwards began a series of God-anointed sermons in his church in Northhampton, Massachusetts. Edwards was one of two key individuals the Lord used mightily during that revival now called the Great Awakening. An intellectual giant who had begun the study of Latin at age six, entered Yale at thirteen, and graduated at sixteen, Edwards with his preaching touched off what would prove to be a major work of the Spirit.

Yet as one writer put it, this was "just a flicker of greater things to come" when the second key figure, twenty-five-year-old George Whitefield, a colleague of the Wesley's in England, burst upon the American scene. "If Edwards touched off the fire, Whitefield swept the white-hot flames throughout all of New England and into the south."[2]

But even before revival spread like wildfire, the early signs of revival were appearing in churches such as the one Edwards pastored. Christ's presence was keenly felt.

In his prolific writings, Edwards touches on specifics, such as:

"Everyone [was] earnestly intent on the public worship"—measurement number one:

> It has been observable that there has been scarce any part of divine worship wherein good men amongst us have had grace so drawn forth, and their hearts so lifted up in the ways of God as in singing his praises. . . . They were evidently wont to sing with unusual elevation of heart and voice, which made the duty pleasant indeed.[3]

Regarding the importance of Christian love in this colonial spiritual regenesis, Edwards writes, "If the spirit at work among a people operates as a spirit of love, it is a sure sign that it is the spirit of God"—measurement number two.

In another place, Edwards asks, "Would the devil make us more careful to discern what is sinful and more careful to guard against it? This is what has been happening. Why then do people question that the spirit that has been operating is any but the spirit of God?"—holiness, measurement number three.

God's people getting involved in ministry is the fourth measurement we have listed. Of this, Edwards affirms, "The congregation was alive in God's service."

During the Great Awakening, the written and spoken Word came alive—revival measurement number five. Edwards again:

> Every hearer [was] eager to drink in the words of the minister as they came from his mouth; the assembly in general were, from time to time, in tears while the word was preached; some weeping with sorrow and distress, others with joy and love, others with pity and concern for the souls of their neighbors.[4]

As the Lord moved there was a boldness in prayer requesting that the Spirit come in even greater power—measurement number six. To continue the awakening, Edwards and others called for concerts of prayer "every quarter of the year."

THE BEST OF TIMES

It is estimated that during the Great Awakening there were between twenty-five thousand and fifty thousand converts—measurement number seven. Percentage-wise that would be roughly equivalent to twenty-five million converts on the American scene today!

Christ was present in His church during these historic days, and evidences of this were worship and love and holiness and service and obedience to Scripture and prayer and outreach evangelism—all the themes which have been covered in this book so far. But there is one last ingredient which hasn't been developed. Measurement number eight is an intense sense of well-being. During revival, God's people believe that what is going on is truly life as it should be lived, that no better life is possible than one lived in the very presence of the risen Christ.

On 21 December 1743, Edwards wrote,

Ever since the great work of God that was wrought here about nine years ago, there has been a great, abiding alteration in this town in many respects. There has been vastly more religion kept up in the town, among all sorts of persons, in religious exercises, and in common conversation, than used to be before. There has remained a more general seriousness and decency in attending the public worship. —I suppose the town has been in no measure so free from vice, —for any long time together, for this sixty years, as it has this nine years past. There has also been an evident alteration with respect to a charitable spirit to the poor.[5]

William Cooper, another man of God who witnessed the Great Awakening, wrote concerning this sense of well-being:

Behold, the Lord whom we have sought, has suddenly come to his temple. The dispensation of grace we are now under, is certainly such as neither we nor our fathers have seen, and in some circumstances so wonderful, I believe there has not been the like since after our Lord's ascension. The apostolic times seem to have returned upon us.[6]

When the people of the church again know the presence of the Lord, they experience the best of days. The point is so obvious. Yet for some reason it helps to spell it out.

Is it a disadvantage or an advantage for individuals to have Jesus as a close friend? Is it the sinner or the saint who knows the good life? Is Christ's yoke heavy or is it light? I'm not asking for answers like those you might give on a Bible quiz, but for where you are in your heart of hearts. Does the pretender to the throne know what's best for you, or is the path of joy the one mapped out by your true King?

Regarding the church, have the glory days been when God's people selfishly figured out what they wanted and pursued it, or when they were obedient to Christ's commands? Did distancing itself from the divine presence bring the church freedom or bondage? When life returned, when there was revival, was the result cursing or blessing?

How fascinating it has been in my studies of literature on awakenings to read the remarks of people in the midst of revival. Their comments always convey excitement, delight, gratitude, and even a touch of awe. It's like you can almost conclude what is said each time with the words, "This has to be the best life has to offer."

I am aware that spiritual awakenings can't be humanly engineered, but that doesn't prohibit us from attempting to experience a little of the classic characteristics of revival—the worship, the love, the sense of victory over sin, the delight in service, and so on. Experiencing some of these realities could create a hunger for another such outpouring, leading to a common dedication of ourselves to praying boldly for God's work among us.

How desperately our day needs this! I believe that even sampling Christ's presence in the church will create a longing for more and more of the same.

So we must learn how to worship and teach one another how to delight in it. Buy a hymnal. Even if you can't sing, read and reread the songs, especially those addressed to Christ.

Allow the hymns about His church to capture your heart.

Work at making it a habit to extend King's love to others. Put away petty attitudes, jealousies, gossip, neglect.

Don't give an inch to the enemy. Determine to be Christ-like in your attitude regarding sin.

Never stop improving your ability to serve your Lord. Surprise Him with all you can do on His behalf!

As Paul wrote to Timothy, be a master handler of God's Word. But don't just study it, obey it.

Develop a more mature system of prayer than just keeping a running list in your head. Start a journal or a prayer notebook.

Go ahead. Share with someone else what Christ means to you. Tell somebody.

Do the things you would do were Jesus bodily present, and see if you don't say, "For me, life is better now than it has been for a long time. I never thought it could be so good." Enjoy spiritual well-being.

When properly understood, revival is nothing to fear. If the word implied unchecked emotionalism, I could understand why people would react against it; but emotionalism is an unfair description More than anything else, revival means that Christ has again drawn near to His people, and that's always a happening that's wonderful for those who love Him. How can life be better than when it is infused with Christ's divine presence?

I believe revival is what all true Christians desire, even if they aren't aware of what their longing is called. After all, revival is the chance to start all over again and to do it right this time. It's a brand new beginning—a regenesis—for the individual, for the family, for the church, for the community, for the nation. What could possibly be better than that? I know I long for it.

At my office at The Chapel of the Air, there's a large *National Geographic* map stretched across the top of my desk under the protective glass. It includes most of Canada, all the United States, and the top portion of Mexico. I've become very familiar with it because I do so much work at that desk.

When I work at home, my small study is in the very center of our house. The room is only seven by eleven feet, but I like it. The best feature is that, by closing the study door, I can shut myself off from the demands of my more immediate world and just be alone there with the Lord. Everyone should have such a room—a prayer room, a family chapel.

Sometimes in the study at home when I close my eyes in prayer, the outline of the map from the office desk returns to mind. Then it is as though, when I kneel to pray, I'm viewing all of North America, and my normal concern is intensified for this massive geographic area into which we broadcast each day of the week but Sunday.

Often I visualize dark, angry clouds hovering over much of our continent. Even so, I'm able to discern what appear to be tiny fires in various places. Unfortunately there aren't many, and they're widely separated. While some barely flicker, the last embers of a once-bright blaze, others still burn with great constancy. But the longer I pray, the more tiny flashes I'm able to find. This is not unlike observing the heavens at night; the longer one looks, the greater the number of stars which can be seen.

In my vision of this strategic part of earth, I'm aware that these bright lights are churches where the life of Christ is manifested. "But can't there be more?" my heart whispers. Those threatening clouds will extinguish some of the weaker fires.

As if in response to my prayers, some flames actually leap up and burn more brightly—small in number, yes, but intense and pure. Alas, the adverse elements begin to move in concentration against them. Watching this dark power forming and knowing what is soon to be unleashed, I become discouraged. "Why even pray? These burning testimonies haven't a chance."

But wait! Beneath the onslaught of foul winds, sparks now dance out from the flames under attack. Here now, over there again, and then in new places they spring up. Defiantly

the little fires seem to shout to the storms, "All your bluster-
ing will be counterproductive, utterly self-defeating, only
fanning holy flames."

This imaginative development encourages my intercession. "More fires," I pray. "God, if we just had more fires—
hundreds, thousands of them, even tens of thousands. With
more fires, the possibility for holy flame in these lands becomes reachable." I strategize: "There need to be ignition
points everywhere, each catching and spreading and feed-
ing one another, so many there won't be enough clouds and
contrary winds or hostile rains to extinguish all the blazing
lights."

Then, as if in response to my thought, which hardly takes
long enough time to be called a prayer, numbers of areas
blaze brighter—more starlike points flame, north and south,
east and west—further increasing my faith. "Look, it's happening, Lord!" I cry. "Please keep the miracle alive!"

"Come and pray with me," I call in my prayers to unseen
friends—brothers, and sisters. I don't know many of them
by name, but I do know our hearts and minds are as one.
"Do you see what I'm seeing?"

In my spirit I hear their voices join with mine; soon their
intercession can be observed. For the first time a concentration of flames combines with another nearby. The action is
dramatic, lighting the area with intense heat. Cheers unite
our prayer vigil. All of us are caught up with the intense
work of intercession, and in some strange way we know that
what's happening is fueled by a force totally beyond us.

I attempt to identify cities which might be involved.
Denver. Minneapolis. Toronto. Isn't that Baltimore? This
must be Phoenix down here. Oh, if only a true phoenix is
alight—a flaming new spiritual life rising out of earlier ashes.

The warfare intensifies. A great hostile wind now whips
and blows against an area representing several counties, and
the strong fires burning there dim. But when the contrary
force has spent itself, the incendiary fellowship flares
again. Before long it is brighter than before and noticeably
expanded.

With this, a turning point has been reached, a key defeat wielded against the haters of holy fire. And *suddenly,* as though a signal has been flashed, there is a dramatic acceleration of flame. New burning torches appear, brighter ones, everywhere on the continent—Canada, most of the States, even areas of Mexico.

I gasp, "Lord, another holy conflagration that won't burn out for years to come. O may it be so!"

The time is crucial. To insure victory, I and my prayer partners must stay at our prayer posts. "Before too long," I tell God, "it should all catch. It's going to be impossible to stop what's happening. Come now, you foul winds, blow some more! You only fan our flames!" And then—

Well, the phone rings.

Or someone opens the study door and says, "Dad, did you remember I need a ride to my lesson?"

Or I hear, "Sweetheart, can you please feed the dog tonight? I did it yesterday."

—And I'm back, back into the more immediate of the two worlds in which I live.

But I don't forget. I don't ever forget what I saw when my eyes were closed and I knelt over North America in my prayers. I cannot forget this vision of what still could be.

Personally, my heart is hot for more of the things of the Lord. With my wife, Karen, I believe our marriage has been permanently branded by Christ. I trust that we display His flaming mark on our lives. Nor do we feel alone; we're joined by countless others, couples and singles, who pray,

> Breathe on me, breath of God,
> Till I am wholly Thine,
> Till all this earthly part of me
> glows with thy fire divine.[7]

But the vision calls for more than just individuals or couples or families here and there. It requires the vast extended people of God, the church, to experience the sacred flames

So often in Scripture, God demonstrated His presence by fire. To Abraham it was a smoking pot and a flaming torch as God's Spirit passed between the two halves of this man's sacrifices. To Moses it was a burning bush. To the children of Israel fleeing from Egypt, the Lord was in the pillar of fire; in their worship, God's presence was at the altar in the time when the burnt offerings were made. Elijah was called home to God in a chariot of fire drawn by horses of fire. Elisha asked God to give His servant eyes to see the mountains full of horses and chariots of fire. At Pentecost, tongues of fire rested on each gathered in that special room when they were shaken with the coming of the Holy Spirit.

And I believe, in the end time prior to the return of His Son, that our Lord desires His church once again to know the best of times and to burn brightly in sacred revival flames.

May it be so. I pray on.

For Discussion and Reflection

1. Some people say the Bible predicts the world will get worse and worse before Jesus returns; therefore, we shouldn't expect another great revival. Do you agree or disagree?

2. Many Christians have positive feelings about revival personalities such as Luther, Wesley, Finney, Moody, and so on, but they have negative feelings about revival itself. Why is this?

3. When is the last time you recall hearing someone in your church pray for revival?

4. What changes would be made if Christ became your permanent house guest? Resaid, what would it be like if you became more and more aware of the presence of Christ in your home? Same question again, how would revival affect your home life?

5. In what ways have revival truths started to affect your personal life? Name a specific area where the Lord is presently wanting improvement. Do you need help in knowing how to make the necessary changes?

Readings

"TIMES OF REFRESHING from the presence of the Lord." The thought surely opens up for us a mental vista of the possibilities of blessing through seeking God's presence—possibilities often hidden by the thick clouds of our own great ignorance. To be in the presence of the Lord is to be revived. When a community of believers is brought low before the presence of the Lord, when the very air that they breathe appears to be supercharged with the sense of His presence—that is the beginning of revival. It *is* revival. . . .

I have witnessed many revivals of God's people—both individuals and companies. The Holy Spirit's working always brought a fulness of joy. Cups ran over. Worries disappeared. When Love, and Joy, and Peace came in at the door, Misery went up the chimney, search parties failing to locate it afterwards. "Delight thyself in the Lord, and He shall give thee the desires of thine heart" (Ps. 37, 4).

—J. Edwin Orr, Times of Refreshing: 10,000 Miles of Miracle—
Through Canada, pp. 118–119

— ◆ —

THE CRUCIAL TEST of the genuineness of the 1800 Awakening was not the size of the crowds or the degree of excitement, but the spiritual fruits. Dr. George A. Baxter affirmed:[8]

On my way, I was informed by settlers on the road that the character of Kentucky was entirely changed, and that they were as remarkable for sobriety as they had formerly been for dissoluteness and immorality. And indeed I found Kentucky to appearances the most moral place I had ever seen. A profane expression was hardly ever heard. A religious awe seemed to pervade the country. Upon the whole, I think that the revival in

Kentucky the most extraordinary that has ever visited the Church of Christ.

—J. Edwin Orr, *The Eager Feet:
Evangelical Awakenings, 1790–1830*, p. 00

— ◆ —

THE CHARACTERISTICS of the work of grace [in Scotland] during the years 1839 to 1841, were thus noticed in an address from Mr. [William C.] Burns's own pen, bearing the date September 1, 1841:

'Perhaps you have heard of the wonderful things which the great God has been doing for us in Scotland. The servants of Satan have reviled God's blessed work; and I wish to tell you something of the truth about it. You know that many people come from the church the same as they went to it; the Word does not touch their consciences, and they remain under the power of sin and Satan, of death and hell. This used to be very much the way among us until lately; but the God of love has visited us, and poured out his life-giving Spirit upon the dead souls of men. In some places you might see the solemn sight of hundreds weeping for their sins, and seeking to give up their hearts to Jesus. And, ah! what a sweet change has taken place on many! The high looks of the proud have been brought down; dead formalists have become living Christians; worshippers of Mammon have been changed into lovers of God; the blasphemous tongues of the profane have been made to sing God's praise; drunkards have cast from them the cup of devils, and have taken the cup of salvation; unclean persons, who used to be the slaves of lust, the drudges of the devil, the very dregs of humankind, are now sitting at the feet of Jesus; and some, who were ringleaders in every form of sin, are bold now and open, and unflinching in the service of Christ, even as once they were shameless, brazen-faced, and steel-hearted in the service of the Wicked One. Many, who formerly were dead in sin, are now living in the grace of Jesus, in the love of God, in the communion of the Spirit, and in the hope of heaven!'

At the present time, when many are stirred up to lay hold on the God of Pentecost, there is a special interest and pleasure in looking back to those days of his right hand—days which, during succeeding times of deadness, it became almost saddening to recall.

The instruments then employed were ever made to feel that the entire power which accompanied the word resided in God the Holy Ghost, honoured as the living Jehovah, specially addressed in believing prayer, and shed forth in glorious power. Mr. Burns was only in his twenty-fifth year in 1839–40, and did indeed ascribe all the glory of the effects of his preaching to God alone. The written Word was magnified. Sometimes inquirers would tell that what had been used to awaken them was the Scripture read or the psalm sung. The sanctuary was felt to be the very house of God. Reasons and excuses for absence, at other times insurmountable, how quickly they gave way! Daily labour was got over in time; and through the winter dark, or by the moonlight on the snow, eager hundreds were pressing to its gates, some still like burdened CHRISTIAN, others rejoicing in the Savior newly found, and careless ones, who came from curiosity alone, had to sit and think, silent and still, for an hour in the crowd, till the service began. That solemn stillness was often followed by such requests for prayer as those which have become so common now—believers asking prayer for unconverted relatives, and awakened sinners asking it for themselves.

—M. F. Barbour, editor, *Revival Sermons:*
Notes of Addresses by William C. Burns, pp. 8–10

— ◆ —

A CONVERT IN Rochester, New York, left a description of [Charles] Finney's revival ministry [1842] in that city. . . . He wrote: "The whole community was stirred. Religion was the topic of conversation, in the house, in the shop, in the office, and on the street. . . . The only theater in the city was converted into a livery stable; the only circus into a soap and candle factory. Grog shops were closed; the Sabbath was honored; the sanctuaries were thronged with happy worshipers; a new impulse was given to every philanthropic enterprise; the fountains of benevolence were opened, and men lived to do good."

The report continues: "It is worthy of special notice that a large number of leading men of the place were among the converts—the lawyers, the judges, physicians, merchants, bankers, and master mechanics. These classes were more moved from the very first than any other. Tall oaks were bowed as by the blast of the hurricane. . . .

"It is not too much to say that the whole character of the city was changed by that revival," wrote this eye-witness. "Most of the leaders of society being converted, and exerting a controlling influence in social life, in business, and in civil affairs, religion was enthroned as it has been in few places. . . . Even the courts and the prisons bore witness to its blessed effects. There was a wonderful falling off in crime. The courts had little to do, and the jail was nearly empty for years afterward."

—V. Raymond Edman, *They Found the Secret: Twenty Transformed Lives That Reveal a Touch of Eternity*, p. 57

OUR RELIGION IS like fire, again, because of *its tremendous energy and its rapid advance.* Who shall be able to estimate the force of fire? Our forefathers standing on this side of the river, as they gazed many years ago upon the old city of London wrapped in flame, must have wondered with great astonishment as they saw cottage and palace, church and hall, monument and cathedral, all succumbing to the tongue of flame. It must be a wonderful sight, if one could safely see it, to behold a prairie rolling along its great sheets of flame, or to gaze upon Vesuvius when it is spouting away at its

utmost force. When you deal with fire, you cannot calculate;
you are among the imponderables and the immeasureables.
I wish we thought of that when we are speaking of religion.
You cannot calculate concerning its spread. How many years
would it take to convert the world? asks somebody. Sir, it
need not take ten minutes, if God so willed it; because as
fire, beyond all reckoning, will sometimes, when circumstances are congenial, suddenly break out and spread, so will
truth. Truth is not a mechanism—and does not depend upon
engineering. A thought in one mind, why not the same
thought in fifty? That thought in fifty minds, why not in fifty
thousand? The truth which affects a village, and stirs it from
end to end, why not a town, a city, why not a nation? why
not all nations? God may, when he wills it, bring all human
minds into such a condition that one single text such as this,
"This is a faithful saying, and worthy of all acception, that
Christ Jesus came into the world to save sinners," may set all
hearts on a blaze. . . . I can believe anything about fire. Let
a man tell me that in a house just now a bundle of rags have
begun to burn; let him tell me in five minutes that the shop is
on fire; let him tell me in five minutes more that it is blazing
through the shutters, or that the next story is burning, or that
the roof is coming in, I could believe it all. Fire can do anything. So with the gospel of Jesus; given but an earnest
preacher, given but the truth fully declared, given an earnest
people, determined to propagate the gospel, and I can understand a nation converted to God, ay, and all the nations of
the earth suddenly shaken with the majesty of truth.

—C. H. Spurgeon, *The Metropolitan Tabernacle Pulpit: Sermons
Preached and Revised by C. H. Spurgeon During the Year 1869,* pp. 81–82

— ◆ —

SEND THE FIRE

Thou Christ of burning, cleansing flame,
    Send the fire!
Thy Blood-bought gift today we claim,
    Send the fire!
Look down and see this waiting host,
Give us the promised Holy Ghost,
We want another Pentecost,
    Send the fire!

God of Elijah, hear our cry!
   Send the fire!
Oh, make us fit to live or die,
    Send the fire!
To burn up every trace of sin,
To bring the light and glory in,
The revolution now begin,
    Send the fire!

'Tis fire we want, for fire we plead,
    Send the fire!
The fire will meet our ev'ry need,
    Send the fire!
For daily strength to do the right,
For grace to conquer in the fight,
For power to walk the world in white,
    Send the fire!

To make our weak hearts strong and brave,
    Send the fire!
To live a dying world to save;
    Send the fire!
Oh, see us on Thy alter lay
Our lives, our all, this very day;
To crown the off'ring now, we pray,
    Send the fire.

—General William Booth,
in Ted S. Rendall, *Fire in the Church,* p 96

Sources for Readings

The following are full listings for all books quoted from in the Readings sections of this book. For a fascinating and varied picture of what revival is like, I encourage you to look them up!

Bainton, Roland H. *The Church of Our Fathers.* New York: Charles Scribner's Sons, 1950.

Barbour, M. F., editor. *Revival Sermons: Notes of Addresses by William C. Burns.* Carlisle, PA: The Banner of Truth Trust, 1980.

Bennett, William W. *The Great Revival Which Prevailed in the Southern Armies During the Late Civil War Between the States of the Federal Union.* Harrisonburg, VA: Sprinkle Publications, 1976.

Coleman, Robert E. *Dry Bones Can Live Again: Revival in the Local Church.* Old Tappan, NJ: Fleming H. Revell Company, 1960.

Coleman, Robert E., editor. *One Divine Moment: The Asbury Revival.* Old Tappan, NJ: Fleming H. Revell, 1970.

Culpepper, C. L. *The Shantung Revival.* Atlanta: Crescendo Book Publications, 1971.

Dayton, Donald W. *Discovering an Evangelical Heritage.* New York: Harper & Row Publishers, 1976.

Demaray, Donald E., editor. *Devotions and Prayers of John Wesley.* Grand Rapids, MI: Baker Book House, 1957.

Editors of *Christian Life* magazine. *America's Great Revivals: A Compilation of Articles.* Minneapolis: Dimension Books, Bethany Fellowship, 1970.

Edman, V. Raymond. *They Found the Secret: Twenty Transformed Lives That Reveal a Touch of Eternity.* Grand Rapids, MI: Zondervan Publishing House, 1960.

Finney, Charles G. *Revival Lectures.* Old Tappan, NJ: Fleming H. Revell Company.

Foster, K. Neill. *Revolution of Love.* Minneapolis: Bethany Fellowship, 1973.

Gesswein, Armin R. *With One Accord in One Place.* Harrisburg, PA: Christian Publications, 1978.

Gibbs, A. P. *Worship: The Christian's Highest Occupation.* Kansas City: Walterick Publishers.

Greenfield, John. *When the Spirit Came: The Story of the Moravian Revival of 1727.* Minneapolis: Bethany House, 1975.

Griffiths, Alison. *Fire in the Islands!: The Acts of the Holy Spirit in the Solomons.* Wheaton, IL: Harold Shaw Publishers, 1977.

Hoffman, Fred W. *Revival Times in America.* Boston: W. A. Wilde Company, 1956.

Kaiser, Walter C., Jr. *Quest for Renewal: Personal Revival in the Old Testament.* Chicago: Moody Press, 1986.

Lovelace, Richard F. *Dynamics of Spiritual Life: An Evangelical Theology of Renewal.* Downers Grove, IL.: Inter-Varsity Press, 1979.

Lutzer, Erwin W. *Flames of Freedom.* Chicago: Moody Press, 1976.

Matthews, David. *I Saw the Welsh Revival.* Chicago: Moody Bible Institute, 1951.

Orr, J. Edwin. *Campus Aflame: Dynamic of Student Religious Revolution: Evangelical Awakenings in Collegiate Communities.* Glendale, CA: Regal Books, 1971.

Orr, J. Edwin. "Cleanse Me." *Inspiring Hymns.* Grand Rapids, MI: Zondervan Publishing House, 1951.

Orr, J. Edwin. *The Eager Feet: Evangelical Awakenings, 1790–1830.* Chicago: Moody Press, 1975.

Orr, J. Edwin. *Evangelical Awakenings in Southern Asia.* Minneapolis: Bethany House, 1975.

Orr, J. Edwin. *Times of Refreshing: 10,000 Miles of Miracle—Through Canada.* Grand Rapids, MI: Zondervan Publishing House, 1936.

Pollock, J. C. *Moody: A Biographical Portrait of the Pacesetter in Modern Mass Evangelism*. New York: The Macmillan Company, 1963.

Ravenhill, Leonard. *America Is Too Young to Die*. Minneapolis: Bethany House, 1979.

Ravenhill, Leonard. *Revival: God's Way*. Minneapolis: Bethany House, 1983.

Ravenhill, Leonard. *Revival Praying*. Minneapolis: Bethany Fellowship, 1962.

Rendall, Ted S. *Fire in the Church*. Chicago: Moody Press, 1974.

Sheldon, Charles M. *In His Steps* (a novel). Springdale, PA: Whitaker House, 1979.

Spurgeon, C. H. *The Metropolitan Tabernacle Pulpit: Sermons Preached and Revised by C. H. Spurgeon During the Year 1869*. London: Passmore and Alabaster, 1869.

Tarr, Charles R. *A New Wind Blowing*. Anderson, IN: Warner Press, 1972.

Torrey, R. A. *Why God Used D. L. Moody*. Chicago: Moody Press, 1923.

Tozer, A. W. *Worship: The Missing Jewel of the Evangelical Church*. Harrisburg, PA: Christian Publications, 1961.

Wallis, Arthur. *Revival: The Rain from Heaven*. Old Tappan, NJ: Fleming H. Revell, 1979.

Notes

Chapter 1

1. Bennet Tyler, compiler, *New England Revivals As They Existed at the Close of the Eighteenth and the Beginning of the Nineteenth Centuries* (Boston: Massachusetts Sabbath School Society, 1846, reprinted Wheaton, IL: Richard Owen Roberts Publishers, 1980), p. 7.

2. Ibid., pp. 150–152, 154, 159.

3. Stormie and Michael Omartian, "The Trumpet of Jesus." Used by permission; see acknowledgments for full notice.

Chapter 2

1. Gerhard Tersteegen (1697–1769), composite translation, in A. W. Tozer, ed., *The Christian Book of Mystical Verse* (Harrisburg, PA: Christian Publications, 1963), pp. 60–61. Used by permission; see acknowledgments for full notice.

2. Edward Perronet, "All Hail the Power of Jesus' Name."

3. Charles G. Finney, *Revival Lectures* (Old Tappan, NJ: Fleming H. Revell Company), p. 7.

4. Graham Kendrick, *Learning to Worship As a Way of Life* (Minneapolis: Bethany House, 1984), p. 23. Used by permission; see acknowledgments for full notice.

5. V. Raymond Edman, *Out of My Life* (Grand Rapids, MI: Zondervan Publishing House, 1961), pp. 118–19. Used by permission; see acknowledgments for full notice.

6. Ibid., p. 220.

Chapter 3

1. David Otis Fuller, ed. and comp., *Valiant for the Truth* (New York: McGraw Hill Book Company, 1961), p. 299.

2. Oswald J. Smith, ed., *David Brainerd: His Message for Today* (London: Marshall, Morgan and Scott, 1949), p. 60. Used by permission; see acknowledgments for full notice.

3. Ibid., p. 66.
4. Ibid., p. 67.
5. Ibid., pp. 69–70.
6. Ibid., pp. 71, 73.
7. Ibid., p. 74.
8. Ibid., pp. 74–75.
9. K. Neill Foster, *A Revolution of Love* (Minneapolis: Bethany Fellowship, 1973), pp. 13–14. Used by permission; see acknowledgments for full notice.

Chapter 4
1. Finney, *Revival Lectures*, p. 8.
2. Reported by Duncan Campbell, leader of this revival, as quoted in Arthur Wallis, *In the Day of Thy Power* (London: Christian Literature Crusade), p. 124.
3. See W. H. Foote, *Sketches of Virginia*, p. 427; *Sketches of North Carolina*, chapter XXVII: "Rev. James McGready and the Revival of 1800."
4. James McGready, "A Short Narrative of the Revival of Religion in Logan County," *New York Missionary Magazine*, 1802, pp. 74–75, 151–155, 192–197, 234–236.
5. Letter of James McGready to Dr. Thomas Coke, *Methodist Magazine*, London 1803, pp. 181–184.
6. *New York Missionary Magazine*, 1802, pp. 151–155.

Chapter 5
1. Isaac Watts (1674–1748), "Jesus Shall Reign Where'er the Sun."
2. William P. Merrill (1867–1954), "Rise Up, O Men of God."
3. Ibid.

Chapter 8
1. Finney, *Revival Lectures*, p. 7.
2. Don Francisco, "Got to Tell Somebody." Used by permission; see acknowledgments for full notice.
3. Ibid.
4. Ibid.

Chapter 9

1. Fred W. Hoffman, *Revival Times in America* (Boston: W. A. Wilde Company, 1956), p. 42.

2. Editors of *Christian Life* magazine, *America's Great Revivals: A Compilation of Articles* (Minneapolis: Dimension Books, Bethany Fellowship, 1970), p. 12.

3. Jonathan Edwards, *A Faithful Narrative of the Surprising Word of God* (Grand Rapids, Baker Book House, 1979), p. 17.

4. Ibid., p. 17.

5. Ibid., page number unavailable.

6. William Cooper, source unknown.

7. Edwin Hatch (1835–1889), "Breathe on Me, Breath of God."

8. J. M. King, *A History of the South Carolina Baptists*, p. 155.

Acknowledgments

Every effort has been made to trace the ownership of copyrighted material used in this book and to secure permission for its use. Should there be any inadvertent error or omission, the author and publisher will be pleased to make the necessary corrections in future printings. Thanks are due to the following for permission to reprint copyrighted material:

See This House Music and Word Music for "The Trumpet of Jesus," Words by Stormie Omartian/Music by Michael Omartian. © Copyright 1981 by See This House Music (Admin. by Word Music) and Word Music (A Div. of WORD, INC.). All rights reserved. International Copyright Secured. Used by permission.

The Banner of Truth Trust, for selection from *Revival Sermons: Notes of Addresses by William C. Burns.*

Bethany House Publishers, Minneapolis, Minnesota, 55438, for selections from: *When the Spirit Came,* by John Greenfield, published and copyright 1975, Bethany House Publishers; *Evangelical Awakenings in Southern Asia,* by J. Edwin Orr, published and copyright 1975, Bethany House Publishers; *Learning to Worship As a Way of Life,* by Graham Kendrick, published and copyright 1984, Bethany House Publishers; *Revolution of Love,* by K. Neill Foster, published and copyright 1973, Bethany House Publishers; *America Is Too Young to Die,* by Leonard Ravenhill, published and copyright 1979; Bethany House Publishers; *Revival: God's Way,* by Leonard Ravenhill, published and copyright 1983, Bethany House Publishers.

The Benson Company, for "Got to Tell Somebody," by Don Francisco. Copyright © 1979 by New Pax Music Press/ ASCAP. All rights reserved. Used by permission of the Benson Company, Nashville, TN.

Christian Publications, 3825 Hartzdale Drive, Camp Hill, PA 17011, for selection from *Worship: The Missing Jewel in the Evangelical Church*, by A. W. Tozer and *The Christian Book of Mystical Verse*, by A. W. Tozer.

Donald Dayton, for selection from his book, *Discovering an Evangelical Heritage*.

Alison Griffiths, for selection from her book, *Fire in the Islands*.

Home Mission Board, Southern Baptist Convention, for selection from *The Shantung Revival*, by C. L. Culpepper.

Inter-Varsity Press, for selection from *Dynamics of Spiritual Life: An Evangelical Theology of Renewal*, by Richard F. Lovelace, © 1979 by Intervarsity Christian Fellowship of the USA, and used by permission of Inter-Varsity Press, PO Box 1400, Downers Grove, IL 60515.

Marshall, Morgan & Scott Publications/Pickering & Inglis Ltd., for selection from *David Brainerd: His Message for Today*, ed. by Oswald J. Smith.

Moody Press, for selection from *I Saw the Welsh Revival*, by David Matthews; *Quest for Renewal: Personal Revival in the Old Testament*, by Walter C. Kaiser, Jr.; *Flames of Freedom*, by Erwin W. Lutzer; *Why God Used D. L. Moody*, by R. A. Torrey.

Ted S. Rendall, for selection from his book, *Fire in the Church*.

Fleming H. Revell, for selections from *Revival: The Rain from Heaven*, by Arthur Wallis; *One Divine Moment: The Asbury Revival*, ed. by Robert E. Coleman; and *Dry Bones Can Live Again: Revival in the Local Church*, by Robert E. Coleman.

Charles Scribner's Sons, for selection from *The Church of Our Fathers*, by Ronald H. Bainton. Copyright 1941 Charles Scribner's Sons; copyright renewed. Copyright 1950 Ronald H. Bainton; copyright renewed. Reprinted with the permission of Charles Scribner's Sons, an imprint of Macmillan Publishing Company.

Sprinkle Publications, for selection from *The Great Revival Which Prevailed in the Southern Armies During the Late Civil War Between the States of the Federal Union*, by William W. Bennett.